CW00370023

SECRET
BARCELONA

Verónica Ramírez Muro - Rocio Sierra Carbonell

WALKING OFF THE BEATEN TRACK

Secret Barcelona is the result of the observation that the range of guidebooks available to residents or frequent visitors to the city all tend to describe the same familiar places. There is almost nothing that will come as a surprise or offer anything new to anyone who knows Barcelona well.

This guide is aimed at such readers, although we hope that it will also please the occasional visitor who wants to depart from the tourist track and take advantage of the often hidden attractions of the city.

Comments about this guide and its contents, as well as information on places we may not have included, are very welcome and will allow us to enrich future editions.

Don't hesitate to write to us:
• E-mail: info@jonglezpublishing.com
• Jonglez publishing, 17, boulevard du Roi,
  78000 Versailles, France

Montaña de Collserola

Montbau

TIBIDABO

Observatorio
Fabra

Vall d'Hebron

Penitents

PLAÇA DE
ALFONSO
COMÍN

*Parqu
Güell*

Vallcarca

*Parque
del Turó
del Putget*

Travesser
de Dalt

Passeig de la Bonanova

General Mitre

Lesseps

GRÀ

SANT GERVASI

Fontana

Ronda

Augusta

Via

PL. DE PRAT
DE LA RIBA

Dalt

Ronda

del

PL. DE JO
CARLES

Diagonal

Diagonal

María Cristina

PL. DE LA
REINA MARÍA
CRISTINA

Zona Universitària

Palau Reial

PL. DE
PIUS XII

Avigunda

Diagonal

Avigunda de Pedralbes

Ronda

del

LES CORTS

EIXAMPLE

les
Corts

Corts

PLAÇA DE
FR. MACIÀ

Carrer del Comte

Provença

Carrer

Les Corts

Camp Nou

Plaça del Centre

Hospital
Clínic

Universi

Entença

de Roma

Carrer

Travessera

Carrer

Via de Carles III

Avigunda de Josep Tarradellas

Estació Central
Barcelona-Sants

Pubilla Cases

Collblanc

Badal

*ESQUERRA
DE L'EIXAMPLE*

Urgell

Univers

Rocafort

Torrassa

de

Estació
Sants

Tarragona

*Parque
J. Miró*

*SANT
ANTONI*

Sant Antoni

RA

Hostafrancs

Sants

PL. de
Sants

Les Arenes

Espanya

Santa Eulàlia

Badal

Poble Sec

Paral

*L'Hospitalet
de Llobregat*

PLAÇA
D'ESPANYA

del

Paral·lel

POBLE SEC

Gran Via de les Corts Catalanes

de

la

Gran Via

*Palau
Nacional*

Passeig de la Zona Franca

Avigunda

MONTJUIC

*Castell
de Montjuic*

Ronda

del

Litt

*Cementerio
de Montjuic*

◄ Aeropuerto Barcelona - El Prat

CONTENTS

EL RAVAL

EIXAMPLE

CONTENTS

WEST

NORTH

EAST

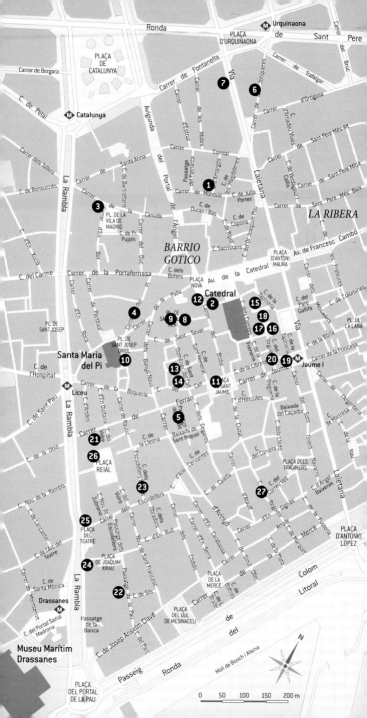

BARRIO GÓTICO

TRAVIS PUPPETS

Carrer d'Amargós, 4
Metro: Catalunya
• Tel: 93 412 6692
• Open Monday to Saturday,
  10.00–14.00 and 16.00–18.00

*Spitting
image*

Since 1977, Teresa Travieso has been making puppets modelled on people's faces. If you agree to pose for a few sessions while you are measured and your vital statistics calculated, you can take away your own image in miniature!

Teresa also works from photographs but the results are not so impressive. Her shop, in one of the narrowest streets of the Barrio Gótico (Gothic quarter), is worth a visit for the intriguing sight of innumerable marionettes hanging from their strings.

She also has puppets for hire and offers a restoration service: she can make them perform the most ingenious movements, for example, dance like Michael Jackson! Her fees depend on the materials used.

SIGHTS NEARBY

A LITTLE-KNOWN VIEWPOINT

Arxiu Històric de la Ciutat de Barcelona
Carrer de Santa Llúcia, 1
Metro: Jaume I
• Tel: 93 318 1195
• Open Monday to Friday, 9.00–20.45
• http://www.bcn.cat/arxiu/arxiuhistoric/

The third floor of the Historic Archive of the City of Barcelona has bay windows overlooking Plaça de la Seu and Barcelona Cathedral. The view is spectacular from this select vantage point, known only to the lucky few.

To reach it, you have to go up to the general reading room, the perfect place for those who like to immerse themselves in historical documents. This venerable institution has acquired all the periodicals of the last 100 years, with an emphasis on those published during the Civil War. The entire collection comprises 13,000 magazines and journals, plus 90,000 books, making it the most comprehensive archive of journalism in Barcelona.

The home of the city archives is a former ecclesiastical residence known as the Casa de l'Ardiaca (Archdeacon's House).

Construction began in the 15th century upon part of the Roman walls. Since then, the building has had several owners and been renovated several times, but it still has its original patio and font at the entrance, now with an Art Nouveau letterbox designed by Lluís Doménech i Montaner.

CLUB ATENEU BARCELONÉS

③

Carrer de la Canuda, 6
Metro: Catalunya • Tel: 93 343 6121 • Open daily 9.00–22.30
• www.ateneubcn.org/
• Members only. Monthly subscription (€21) gives access to all Ateneu
  services: library, meeting rooms, cafeteria
• If you only want to visit the romantic gardens,
  you can ask for a special pass at reception

A secret garden and library

The Sabassona palace was commissioned by Josep Francesc de Llupià, baron of Sabassona, in 1779. Designed by the architect Pau Mas and listed as a national monument, the neoclassical building was renovated several times in the course of the 20th century.

Other than its architectural importance (notably the superb entrance door on Carrer de la Canuda), the palace features the paintings of Françesc Pla ("El Vigatà"), who in the mid-18th century made his name as interior decorator of stately homes and private mansions.

He also designed the romantic garden located 5 metres above street level, a superbly relaxing spot with a wide variety of plants and flowers, in the heart of the Barrio Gótico.

Since 1907 the palace has been home to Ateneu Barcelonés, which defines itself as "a haven of tolerance, liberty and national culture."

Apart from the romantic garden and a collection of artworks, the Ateneu has a fantastic library of over 1,000 m², open to any students and researchers with an interest in Catalonian history, politics, and society.

Recent renovation work has returned the library to the splendour of its early years (it was founded in 1860).

The repository contains over 300,000 volumes, a great number of incunabula, tens of thousands of historical documents, and special editions dating from the 14th to the 18th centuries. It is one of the most important national collections in Spain.

WATERING THE HORSES

The drinking fountains where tourists and local residents come to refresh themselves today were, until the late 1950s, intended for draught animals that pulled the carts carrying merchandise into the city. They were to be found at 77 Vila i Vilá, 40 Carrer del Consell de Cent, and at the junction of Portal de l'Ángel and Carrer del Cucurulla. The oldest (14th century) is the one in Cucurulla.

The errand boys responsible for delivering goods in the port area, and in particular the neighbourhoods of El Born and Poble Nou, would stop at the water troughs to let the animals refresh themselves, usually leaving them tied up while they themselves drank eau-de-vie or wine in the bars nearby.

POLYCLINIC FOR TOYS ④

Carrer del Pi, 3. Galería C, 5
Metro: Liceu
- Tel: 93 317 6554
- Open Tuesday to Saturday, 11.00–13.30
  and 17.00–20.30, and Monday, afternoons only

Dolls'
hospital

J ust like their owners, dolls and teddy bears paid the price of the Civil War. In 1946 a leading Spanish businesswoman, María Rigoll, opened a clinic specializing in mending and reassembling all kinds of toys. Sixty years later, the business is still thriving, thanks to the surgical precision with which she puts her patients back together again.

The boutique-workshop, crammed with legs, heads, furry coats and thousands of miniature clothes, attracts a wide range of customers: most of them are adults trying to recapture their childhood and give a new lease of life to their old friends, or children who want their teddy fixed after the dog has chewed it.

The procedure depends on the material the toy is made from. As a general rule, clothes are made at the clinic and soft toys are sent out to be resewn, some to have new bits added and others to be remodelled. Heads cause particular problems as it is not always easy to find suitable replacements. In many cases, the whole head has to be rebuilt, as we saw in the case of one doll that had been the victim of a voodoo session!

The clinic also runs courses on repairing and personalizing toys. If the clothes a doll is wearing are not to a customer's taste, others can be substituted, and its shoes, hair, and even its eye colour can be changed.

SIGHTS NEARBY

PASSATGE DEL CREDIT ⑤

This narrow passage was the birthplace of Joan Miró in 1893. Other than the discreet plaque commemorating his birth, look for a large archway with a carved wooden roof, sheltering a wall of glass bricks that belonged to the former Gerfa factory.

The modern hotel that stands there today has regrettably failed to take advantage of the original structure. The passage, despite its location in the very heart of the Barrio Gótico, is a peaceful oasis bordered with private houses and plant-filled balconies.

ORATORIA DE LA SANTA FAZ

Carrer de Jonqueres, 27
Metro: Urquinaona
• Open Monday to Friday 10.30–13.30 and 16.00–19.00

In-house chapel

This building, in a row of shops specializing in bed linen, is not particularly eye-catching. Yet it is open to the public, although there is nothing to indicate the small chapel on the first floor.

If only because of its curious location, the Santa Faz (Holy Visage) oratory is one of Barcelona's most extraordinary sites. It used to be a private home, whose owner decided to convert it into an oratory. Over time, he became host and adviser to thousands of worshippers who shared his devotion to the Passion of Christ.

Legend has it that at the sight of Christ carrying the Cross, Saint Veronica wiped the sweat and blood from His face, the image of which was miraculously imprinted on her veil.

Upon the owner's death, the oratory became a public chapel where people can silently worship in a spiritual ambience before Veronica's veil, a replica of the original preserved in Rome.

SIGHTS NEARBY

LUMINOUS CLOCK, VÍA LAIETANA, 69

Since 1935, hundreds of pedestrians a day have stepped on the clock set in the pavement outside No. 69 Vía Laietana. This concrete and quartz timepiece, the work of clockmaker Juan Cabrerizo, is 2 metres in diameter. The numbers are gilded, and the hours and minutes shown by a beam of light. Because the new occupants of the building failed to maintain it, the clock was out of action for a long time; but in 1989, as the commemorative plaque indicates, Cabrerizo's son repaired the mechanism.

MUSEU DEL CALÇAT

Plaça de Sant Felip Neri, 5
Metro: Liceu
• Tel: 93 301 4533
• Open Tuesday to Sunday, 11.00–14.00
• Admission: €2.40

The biggest shoe in the world?

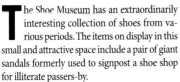

The Shoe Museum has an extraordinarily interesting collection of shoes from various periods. The items on display in this small and attractive space include a pair of giant sandals formerly used to signpost a shoe shop for illiterate passers-by.

Also featured are pointed-toe shoes that the French government banned as dangerous weapons in the 16th century, now back in fashion. You can see shepherd's sandals from the Roman Empire, and filigree metal-trimmed footwear from the 18th, 19th and early 20th centuries. In other showcases are satin pumps, work shoes, Turkish slippers and a musketeer's boots, showing how footgear evolved from the 1st century to the modern age.

Among the most unusual pieces are the cobbler's "last" that was used to make the shoes for the statue of Christopher Columbus at Portal de la Paz, and a replica of the giant shoe (1.22 m) worn by the statue (56 m from the ground to the top of its head).

THE LION OF SAINT MARK, PROTECTOR OF SHOEMAKERS

It is no coincidence that a bas-relief of a lion is carved on the wall of the Shoe Museum: the lion is the symbol of the Evangelist Saint Mark (the Gospel according to Mark begins with images of the desert where the lion reigns supreme), and the saint is also patron of the shoemakers' guild.

In Alexandria, in AD 42, a certain Ananios injured himself while repairing the footwear of the saint, who immediately and miraculously healed him. A legend was born.

The National Art Museum of Catalonia has a fresco from the apse of Sant Climent de Taüll church in the Pyrenees, in which Saint Mark's lion appears. The 12th-century artists were perhaps unfamiliar with lions, as this one looks rather like a bear ...

DISMANTLED STONE BY STONE

The building in which the Shoe Museum is located is the same one that in 1565 became home to the fraternity of Saint Mark the Evangelist and the shoemakers' guild. It used to stand in the Corribia road, before it was bombarded during the Civil War. The building was dismantled stone by stone and rebuilt on its present site during the postwar reconstruction of the Barrio Gótico by architect Adolf Florensa.

SIGHTS NEARBY

TRACES OF SHRAPNEL FROM THE CIVIL WAR

The façades of several building in Plaça de Sant Felip Neri still show the traces of a tragic incident from the Civil War, during which around twenty residents were killed, most of them children. Historians now agree that these are shrapnel impacts from an aerial bombing by Italian planes that took place on 30 January 1938, although after the war Spanish Fascists tried to claim that they were the result of machine-gun fire from street executions carried out by the Communists. In this square, surely one of the most peaceful in the city centre, stands the church where the group of children had found refuge, never thinking that a shell would fall through the roof.

THE MIRACLE OF THE CHURCH OF SANTA MARÍA DEL PI

In the church of Santa María del Pi is a marble plaque dating from 1806 that recounts the story of a miracle.

"On 6 April 1806 came the news of the approbation of the miracles by the servant of God Dr Josep Oriol, for which reason this church was struck by lightning outside; passing by this bridge, the director Josep Mestres fell to the ground thunderstruck without suffering the slightest injury, despite his extraordinary girth, as related in the community archives. This plaque was erected in memory."

THE LIFE OF A SAINT

Josep Oriol is one of the best-loved saints in Barcelona. His life was a series of deprivations marked by his inclination to fast, inspired by a revelation that occurred when he was private tutor to the children of a wealthy family. As he sat down at table one day to share the family meal, his hand became paralysed, which he interpreted as a sign from God.

From then on, Josep Oriol nourished himself only on bread and water, until he died at the age of 52.

On Sundays he added a few herbs to the driest and hardest bread he could find. Throughout his life, he worked among the sick with the greatest humility. He was canonized 200 years later by Pius X.

PUBLIC BATHS

At the corner of Carrer de la Palla, a ceramic plaque bearing the name Banys Nous (New Baths) commemorates the public bathhouse, which offered an essential service between 1160 and 1991. The recently erected plaque can be found near the Baixada de Santa Eulalia. There is, however, another metal plaque dating from 1814 in the Carrer de l'Arc del Teatre, El Raval, which is secured by four nails in the shape of a hand.

ROMAN BARCELONA

In AD 15, Barcelona was known as Colonia *Augusta Faventia Paterna Barcino*, or simply *Barcino*.

The existing city was built over the remains of the Roman one, of which several vestiges can still be seen, the most spectacular of which must be the 3rd-century Roman ramparts.

The brick and mortar walls were almost 2 metres thick with a perimeter of 1,250 metres. The 10 hectare area of enclosed ground was coffin-shaped with four entrances (part of one of the gates is in Carrer de Regomir). The ramparts that can be seen today were constructed on the outer face of the earlier ones, to a height of 8 metres.

They were equipped with sixty-six towers of which very few survive, and unfortunately, not the most spectacular.

If you want to walk round the ramparts, the best place to start is probably Plaça Nova, opposite the cathedral. There, the walls are in a good state of repair. You can also see one of the former gates to the Roman town and the ruins of the aqueducts that brought in fresh water. Roman remains continue along Avinguda de la Catedral, Carrer de la Tapinería, Plaça Ramón Berenguer (where a defensive tower can be seen), and Carrer del Sots Tinent Navarro as far as Plaça dels Traginers.

Then you can follow Carrers del Correu Vell and de Regomir. The best route is to continue via Carrer d' Avinyó, stop awhile at the tower at No. 1 Carrer del Call, turn into Carrer dels Banys Nous then take Carrer de la Palla back to your starting point.

In the Middle Ages, the ancient fortified walls became too confining for the prosperous and expanding city, so King James I of Aragon ordered new walls built, an endeavour that took over a century.

These new walls, which enclosed the principal neighbourhoods of the time, covered an area ten times the size of the Roman city and corresponded to the area now known as the Barrio Gótico.

To complete your tour of Roman Barcelona, we suggest a visit to the basement of the Museu d'Història de la Ciutat (City History Museum), where the largest collection of remains from ancient Barcino is displayed.

THE HIGHEST POINT OF ROMAN BARCELONA

A mill wheel on the ground at No. 10 Carrer del Paradís marks the highest point of the Roman city.

According to certain medieval documents, the hill where the first Romans settled was called Mount Tàber, also known as Mount Miracle. At no more than 16 metres high, it is scarcely noticeable when strolling around the Barrio Gótico. In the 1st century, the extra height did however add to the commanding presence of the temple of Augustus.

SALÓ DE CENT

Plaça de Sant Jaume, 1
Metro: Jaume I
• Admission free Sunday, 10.00–13.30 or by appointment
• Tel: 93 402 7300
• www.bcn.cat

A medieval democratic council

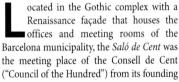

Located in the Gothic complex with a Renaissance façade that houses the offices and meeting rooms of the Barcelona municipality, the *Saló de Cent* was the meeting place of the Consell de Cent ("Council of the Hundred") from its founding in the 13th century until the 18th century. You can book a visit to admire the majestic structure, consisting of four immense arches separated by wooden beams.

This council of one hundred members allowed ordinary workers and artisans the same voting rights as bankers and property owners.

Designed by the architect Pere Llobet in 1360, the *Saló de Cent* was inaugurated in 1373. In 1842, a workers' revolt broke out and the building was bombarded, sustaining serious damage. Renovations were later carried out by Lluís Doménech i Montaner, who successfully competed against Antoni Gaudí for the commission.

At No. 3 Carrer de Regomir stands one of the oldest buildings in Barcelona, a tower dating from the first Roman settlements in the region. Over the centuries, the place was converted into Roman baths, then in the 15th century it became the private residence of a wealthy family. Today it houses a cultural centre.

The name Regomir comes from the Moorish king Gamir, who lived in that street when Louis the Pious (Emperor Louis I of the Franks) conquered the city in 801.

LAST VESTIGE OF THE BARCELONA TEMPLARS
A trace of the headquarters of the Knights Templar of Barcelona, an important medieval chivalrous order, can be seen in Passeig del Timó. This little door, partly destroyed by vandals, used to lead through the Roman ramparts that surrounded the city. The Templars enjoyed this private passage thanks to a concession from James I of Aragon, who throughout his youth had followed the teachings of the order.

SAINT LUCY'S YARDSTICK
Carrer del Bisbe, façade of Capella de Santa Lucia
next to Barcelona Cathedral

*An ancient
unit of length?*

Carved in the stone of an outer corner of the chapel of Santa Lucia is a vertical rod some 1.5 m long. In the 12th century, it was thought to be the standard for a *destre*, an ancient unit of length equivalent to eight palms, six feet, or two strides.

At the time, each kingdom used different measures, and in Barcelona the *destre* was 1.55 m, about the same as Saint Lucy's yardstick, hence the belief that this was a standard unit of length. In fact, it is not quite eight palms long …

Some historians think that the carving indicates the water level before the chapel was built.

Another hypothesis is that it was just a whim of the architect.

WHAT UNITS OF LENGTH WERE USED IN SPAIN BEFORE THE METRE?

One of the most common units of length before the introduction of the metre was the *legua* (league), which measured the distance travelled in an hour by horse or man. This distance generally varied between 4 and 7 kilometres.

In Spain the league was first defined as equal to 5,000 Castilian *varas* (yards), i.e. 4,190 metres, then towards the 16th century as 20,000 Castilian *pies* (feet), equivalent to 5,573 metres.

The *vara*, equivalent to 33 *pulgadas* (inches - around 84 centimetres), was divided into 2 *codos* (cubits) or 4 *palmos* (palms).

The *braza* (fathom), the distance across a man's outstretched arms, was a marine unit of length that eventually fell into disuse as it was inaccurate.

The inch was measured by the breadth of a man's thumb at the base of the nail and the foot was the length of a man's foot.

Other units of measurement used before the official adoption of the metre included the *toesa cuadrada* (area), the *cordel* (length), and the *celemín* and *fanega* (volumes of grain, etc.).

RUINS OF THE SINAGOGA MAYOR ⓭

Carrer de Marlet, 5
Metro: Liceu
• Tel: 93 317 0790 • Open Monday to Saturday 11.00–14.30 and 16.00–19.30
• Admission: €2
• www.calldebarcelona.org

A small but significant synagogue...

Symbolic of El Call, the Jewish quarter within the Barrio Gótico, is the Main Synagogue dating from the 1st century. Part of the original building remains, facing towards Jerusalem.

Despite its name, the Main Synagogue is tiny – only 60 m², as synagogues were not allowed to exceed 80 m² at the time.

There is an exhibition in the synagogue that reconstitutes the ancient Call, overlooking the Roman forum. Also on display are a number of relics, notably the pewter plates used during Passover by Eastern European Jewish families, and a menorah by Majorcan artist Ferrán Aguiló.

The Main Synagogue had not been used for worship since 1391.

Now restored, it is currently run by a group of conservationists (Associació Call de Barcelona) and hosts Jewish celebrations such as bar mitzvahs and marriages.

SIGHTS NEARBY

THE PLAQUE OF SAMUEL ASARDI ⓮

Outside the synagogue is a plaque inscribed in Hebrew. It was discovered in 1820 and dates from the 12th century. The text, "that his name shall never be extinguished, that his light shall burn eternally," was written in tribute to Samuel Asardi, a rabbi who in 1200 gifted a house to charity. As the original plaque was being persistently vandalized it has been transferred to the City History Museum. The one you can see at Carrer de Marlet is a replica.

EL CALL

The word "Call", which comes from the Hebrew *qahal* (assembly), designates the Jewish neighbourhoods of Catalan towns. Barcelona's Jewish quarter extends from the gates of Castell Nou and the Episcopal Palace, which used to form part of the Roman ramparts, between Arc de Sant Ramón, Call, Bisbe and Sant Sever streets. In the mid-12th century it stretched as far as the present church of Sant Jaume, in the area known as *Call Menor* (Little Call). The influence of the Jews of El Call in Barcelona reached its height in the 12th–14th centuries, due to their prosperous businesses as much their role as money-lenders to James I of Aragon and his successors. In 1391, after an anti-Semitic pogrom throughout Spain left thousands of victims, the gates of the Jewish ghetto in Barcelona were torn down. Of the survivors, many were forced to flee and others converted to Christianity. In 1424, all of the remaining Jews were expelled from El Call, and in 1492, from Barcelona and the whole of Spain.

STREETS IN THE BARRIO GÓTICO NAMED AFTER GUILDS

Daguería (cutlers), Agullers (needle makers), Cotoners (cotton weavers), Espasería (gunsmiths), Mirallers (mirror dealers), Corders (rope makers), Fustería (carpenters), Escudellers (shield makers) and Tapinería, where the shoemakers fashioned women's sandals from cork lined with leather and fabric, are just some of the street names in the Barcelona neighbourhood where the medieval guilds settled to ply their trades.

The guilds were family-based organizations or fraternal societies. The three most important of these guilds were the *elois*, the *julians* and the *esteves*, named after their respective patron saints Eloi (Eligius), Julian and Esteve (Stephen). It was not easy to be accepted by a guild, especially as membership was not hereditary.

It was gained by hard work: the apprentices had to respect a whole series of standards and demonstrate their skills in their chosen trade. The tests were difficult as the work had to be exemplary. For example, if a craftsman decided to use materials of inferior quality, the "examiners" who went round the workshops would force him to hang the faulty pieces from the shop door, and that would be the end of his reputation.

Although on a practical level the guilds existed to protect the interests of craftsmen, set prices, regulate relations between apprentice and master, and guarantee the quality of products, these powerful bodies maintained close links with the Church, negotiated special privileges with monarchs, and sent representatives to the Council of the Hundred.

In times of danger, the guilds were responsible for organizing the defence of the city. In other words, their influence was not limited to professional matters but had repercussions at every level of medieval Barcelona society.

Guild members did not only have premises in the same street, they also shared tools and the means of production. Moreover, the concentration of a group of craftsmen in the same area was practical for customers. Legend has it that a blind man wanting to know his whereabouts was guided by the smells emanating from the different workshops.

The bonds between the guilds and the Church were evident in the cults devoted to their respective patron saints. In Spain, Saints Abdon and Sennen were patrons of the gardeners' guild, Saint Peter cf the fishermen, Saint John the Baptist of the tanners, while Saint Eulalia was both the official patron saint of the city and of masons. Doctors and barbers paid tribute to Saints Cosmas and Damian.

The blacksmiths were a special case, because the tools of all the others depended on them, as did weapons and chivalrous artefacts. They were protected by Saint Eloi.

These guilds existed for 600 years, until the mid-19th century when capitalism, and especially massive investment in industrial factories, spelled the end of the ancestral trades.

GUILD SYMBOLS

In the curved wall of the apse in the east wing of Barcelona Cathedral, almost opposite the Marès Museum, are two arresting sculptures. Both of them belong to Saint Stephen's guild, one of the three main medieval guilds, along with those of Saints Eloi and Julian.

They aimed to provide mutual assistance to their members, much like an insurance company today.

These two sculptures allude specifically to the saddlers' guild. The one on the left represents a saddle and a bit, symbols of the craftsmen who made and sold harness.

The second sculpture (below) is a crown of laurels encircling three stone spheres, which commemorates the stoning of Saint Stephen.

Saint Stephen's guild brings together various trades associated with horsemanship and was very influential at the royal court in the 14th and 15th centuries.

The saddlers were highly respected and had their own chapel by the grand altar of the cathedral.

These symbols were carved in this part of the cathedral because it was closest to Carrer de la Frenería where the saddlers used to work.

SAINT STEPHEN, THE FIRST MARTYR

Known as the first Christian martyr, Saint Stephen was one of the seven deacons charged with helping the apostles.

He worked tirelessly to convert great numbers of Jews to the Christian faith. Accused of blasphemy against Moses and against God, he was stoned at the outskirts of Jerusalem.

There seems to be no particular reason why saddlers are associated with Saint Stephen. In fact, throughout its long history their fraternity had taken responsibility for a wide range of other trades, notably painters, lancers and embroiderers.

THE BREASTS OF SAINT AGATHA

Capella de Santa Agata, Museu d'Història de la Ciutat
Plaça del Rei s/n
Metro: Catalunya, Urquinaona, Jaume I, Liceu
• Tel: 93 315 1111
• 1 October to 30 March: open Tuesday to Saturday, 10.00–14.00 and
16.00–19.00; 1 April to 30 September: open Tuesday to Saturday,
10.00–20.00; and throughout the year open Sundays and holidays,
10.00–15.00
• Admission: €6
• www.museuhistoria.bcn.cat

*Cruel
torment*

Built in 1302 by command of James II of Aragon, the Chapel of Saint Agatha is part of the Roman walls.
It is one of the most secluded religious edifices in the city, upstaged by the neighbouring buildings which include the City History Museum, where an archaeological site has been discovered underneath the buildings: 4,000 m^2 of Roman ruins, among which there is a 3rd-century winery. In the chapel, the centerpiece is a painting of Saint Agatha holding up a tray on which are placed her own breasts. A little further on, the *Condestable* Altarpiece, a 15th-century work by Jaume Huguet, evokes the last moments of Jesus' life. To the right of the altar, a small stairway leads to the 16th-century tower of King Martin I (the Humane) of Aragon.
Climbing these stairs, however, demands physical agility in addition to an interest in history.

SAINT AGATHA

Agatha, a pretty and devout daughter of a Sicilian noble family, was propositioned by the Roman senator Quintianus in the 3rd century, at a time when Christians were being persecuted by the Emperor Trajan. Faced by this Christian virgin's categorical refusal of his advances, he subjected her to the cruellest of tortures. First he sent her into a brothel, but miraculously, she emerged still a virgin. Then she was made to suffer a series of other torments, culminating in the mutilation of her breasts. Agatha was consoled by a vision of Saint Peter, who protected her from pain but not from death. In 250, just one year after her passing, Etna erupted and the islanders called on Saint Agatha to stop the flow of lava. Since that day, Agatha has been the patron saint of Catalonia and Sicily, as well as that of women with breast problems.

A BOMB IN THE HISTORY MUSEUM

On the night of 7 November 1893, the young anarchist Santiago Salvador went to the Liceu theatre to see a production of Rossini's opera *William Tell*, with two bombs concealed about his person. One of them killed twenty members of the audience in the orchestra pit. The other failed to detonate and is now on display at the City History Museum.
These circular metal bombs bear the mark of Felice Orsini (1819–1858), an Italian revolutionary who attempted to kill Napoleon III with a similar device, when he too was on his way to the opera.

STREETLAMPS IN PLAÇA DEL REI

Plaça del Rei
Metro: Jaume I

Let there be light ...

In the square beside the History Museum are replicas of three medieval streetlamps (there are another two in Plaça de Santa María del Mar).

These lamps used resin as fuel, which ignited readily, took a long time to burn and gave off a pleasant smell.

That was very important at the time and served the same purpose as incense in church – neutralizing the smell that filled any space where a great number of pilgrims were gathered, in the days before deodorants and shampoos.

Around 1725, this type of oil lamp was still being used in Barcelona. A century later, on the evening of 24 June 1826, the feast day of Saint John, gas lamps lit up for the first time the building that houses the Barcelona stock exchange (Passeig de Gràcia, 19).

From 1842 onwards, the same system began to be used for lighting the Ramblas and other streets and squares.

The following year, the Frenchman Charles Lebon planned the construction of the first gas production plant, the Sociedad Catalana para el Alumbrado por Gas (Catalan Gaslight Company), which provided lighting on an industrial scale, especially in the developing new factories.

Electric light was not generally available in Barcelona before 1904, although the beginnings of the electrical industry go back to 1873. In that year, the Barcelona optician and physician Tomás Dalmau and the engineer Narciso Xifrá inaugurated the first electricity generating plant.

The system worked with four gas-powered motors that drove machines each producing 200 voltamperes.

These supplied electricity to various premises in the city. 1888 saw the installation of the first electric lampposts, which were to coexist with the gas lamps until the mid-20th century.

THE HANGMAN'S HOUSE

It is said that in the Middle Ages, in this square, just opposite Carrer de la Pietat, the hangman lived in a tiny house that must have been renovated scores of times over the years.

All kinds of myths grew up around him, such as the fact that nobody could touch him, not even his tailor. That was why he always wore a sack held together with a piece of rope. Finally the king took pity on him and granted a special dispensation to the royal tailor to take the hangman's measurements and make him a suit of clothes so that he would not cause alarm in the neighbourhood.

LA SALA FEMENINA, MUSEU FREDERIC MARÈS

Plaça de Sant Iu, 5–6
Metro: Jaume I
• Tel: 93 310 5800
• Open Tuesday to Saturday, 10.00–19.00;
  Sundays and public holidays, 10.00–15.00
• Admission: €3
• www.museumares.bcn.es

The world of Romantic women

F rederic Marès was a great collector. Throughout the 98 years of his life, he nurtured his passion for everyday objects in his roles as sculptor, historian, teacher, and defender of the country's artistic heritage.

The most unusual part of the museum that he left is surely the "Ladies' Quarter," displaying hundreds of feminine accessories dating from the 15th to the 19th centuries: fans, combs, boxes, dressmakers' dummies, hats, a whole range of artefacts which reach a level of sophistication that has to be seen to be believed. This room is a true catalogue of past eras and a remarkable testimony to women's daily lives.

Marès, besides collecting toys, automatons, pipes, Christmas cribs, daguerreotypes, and cameras, was a skilled ornamental sculptor. His work can be seen in many places around the streets of Barcelona, such as *Niña encima de un pez* ("Little girl on a fish") at the junction of Gran Vía de les Corts Catalanes and Rambla de Catalunya. He also carried out a number of official commissions, such as the recumbent statues of James I and James II in Majorca Cathedral. Despite appearances, Marès did not come from a wealthy family like so many other renowned collectors. The success of his sculptures allowed him to indulge his passion for collecting that had begun in childhood, when he hoarded toys and chocolate wrappers.

Apart from thousands of these unusual objects, the museum also has an important collection of Spanish religious sculptures dating from the 12th to the 18th centuries.

FORMER SEAT OF THE INQUISITION

On one of the outer walls of the museum there has survived the emblem of the ecclesiastical tribunal of the Inquisition in Barcelona. Inside, in 1542, heretics and converts were judged, tortured, and murdered. A rare reminder of the atrocities of that time, the emblem can be found beside an old doorway (now closed).

THE ANGEL OF PLAÇA DEL ÁNGEL ⑲

Plaça del Ángel, 2
Metro: Jaume I

Saint Eulalia's miracle

At No. 2 Plaça del Ángel stands a curious bronze figure, thought to be an angel. The left arm of this androgynous figure, wingless and bearing a cross on its forehead, is pointing with an outstretched finger to a spot said to be the site of a miracle – the archway in Baixada de la Llibretería, where there used to be a portrait of Saint Eulalia, patron of the city of Barcelona.

Legend has it that in 879 the mortal remains of the saint were being transferred from Santa María del Mar church to the cathedral. Along the way, someone stole one of Eulalia's fingers and, until it was restored, no human force could move the rest of her body.

The sculpture in Plaça del Ángel is a replica.

The original, which dates from 1618, is in the City History Museum. The portrait of Saint Eulalia disappeared at the end of the 19th century.

SIGHTS NEARBY

THE OLDEST SHOP IN TOWN ⑳

Baixada Llibreteria, 7
• Tel: 93 315 2606
• Open Monday to Friday, 9.00–13.30; Saturday, 16.00–19.30

A short distance from Plaça Sant Jaume can be found Cerería Subirá, the oldest shop in Barcelona.

There was a candle supplier here from 1761, although the shop itself was not opened until 1847, and the site has been owned by just two families over the 250 years of its existence. Such is its reputation that the churches of Barcelona now buy half its total output. The other half goes to customers who like decorative candles, which from Disney characters to more sophisticated creations.

Things have not always gone smoothly for Cerería Subirá but it has coped with various setbacks. After the Civil War, not many people could see any beauty in a candle – far from seeming romantic or intimate, candlelight was instead a reminder of a time of restrictions and suffering.

THE FOUNTAIN OF THE KING'S HERBORIUM

㉑

Carrer del Vidre, 1
Metro: Liceu
• Tel: 93 318 0512
• Open Tuesday to Saturday, 10.00–14.00
  and 17.00–20.00

> *Leeches for apoplexy …*

Founded in 1823, the king's herborium has retained (with a few Gothic touches) its décor from the era of Queen Isabella II, designed by the renowned scenographer Francesc Soler i Rovirosa.

On the ground floor of the shop are sea chests from a late 18th-century ship and, on the ceiling, frescoes that are over 100 years old.

Also of note is a sculpture by Fausto Baratta Rossi commemorating Carl Von Linné (Linnaeus), the Swedish botanist who perfected the classification and nomenclature of plants.

The sculpture incorporates a small fountain for keeping leeches, those little creatures that were once used to lower patients' blood pressure if they were likely to have a stroke. It is commonly thought that the bust on top of the leech fountain is that of Charles III, because of the type of wig he is wearing, but it is in fact Linnaeus.

Until 1857, when Isabella II granted the herborium the title "purveyor to the royal household," it was known as La Linneana after the botanist.

Currently, the shop sells 200 types of medicinal plant, ranging from the classic chamomile for daily infusions to mauve for treating respiratory problems, as well as ginkgo biloba for improving the flow of blood to the brain. Other than medicinal plants and herbs, it offers premium quality products such as olive oil, saffron, and honey.

SIGHTS NEARBY

RENT A WORK OF ART

Crea 21 Galerie d'Art
Passatge de la Pau, 14
Metro: Drassanes
• Tel: 93 317 5851
• Open Monday to Friday, 11.00–20.00
• www.crea21.net

If you want to impress friends with remarkable works of art, Crea 21 is the place for you. This exhibition space and art salesroom offers a large catalogue of works for hire, for businesses or for private homes. You can also change your pieces of art as often as you desire.

Other than art for rent, Crea 21 offers a personalized gift service. If you like the work of any particular artist, they can make a piece to order.

HARE KRISHNA TEMPLE

Carrer de N'Aglá, 14, entresuelo B
Metro: Liceu
• Tel: 93 302 5194
• Open daily
• Menu: €7

> **After lunch, you can visit the temple ...**

The Hare Krishna temple opens its dining room everyday to anyone who accepts its conditions: there is no set menu, you eat whatever is on offer that day, but it is strictly vegetarian, consisting of salad, soup, main dish, dessert, and water. No other drinks are available.

The main entrance is very discreet – there is no notice board, just a doorplate. Inside, the ambience is festive, with incense floating in the air and joyful background music.

The dining room has a small terrace and large windows that bathe the place in light.

After lunch, you can visit the temple: a very spacious hall that you must enter barefoot, dominated by a life-size statue of the founder of the world Hare Krishna movement, A.C. Bhaktivedanta Swami Prabhupada. Both the meal and tour are informal, as are the Sunday open days, aimed at attracting new members.

WHO ARE HARE KRISHNA?

The group known as the International Society for Krishna Consciousness (ISKCON) preaches a faith based on traditional Vaishnava Hinduism, practises bhakti yoga, and worships the god Krishna (literally "principal deity"). Inspired by the teaching of the Bengali saint Caitanya Mahaprabhu (1486–1533), the name of the movement comes from the words of the *maja mantra* (main prayer) chanted by its adherents.

In 1966, Abhay Charanaravinda Bhaktivedanta Swami Prabhupada took his teachings to New York, where he set up a base from which to promote and sell his books in airports and on the street, rapidly increasing the number of followers.

Hare Krishna devotees routinely live apart from their families, believe in reincarnation, and refuse to touch alcohol, tea, cigarettes, meat, or eggs. They do not gamble and sex is for reproductive purposes only.

TRACES OF PROSTITUTES

La Rambla, 22 and 24

Streetwalkers'
legacy

The marks worn in the pavement in front of Nos. 22 and 24 La Rambla have a certain historical significance, completely unknown even to most local residents. They were made by the prostitutes who, over a number of years, paced backwards and forwards on this spot, waiting for clients. Over time, the pressure of their heels wore down the marble and left these indentations for posterity. In 1956, prostitution was banned by the authorities and brothels were closed. The girls were thus forced to seek out their clients on the street and especially, as was the case at Nos. 22 and 24, at the doors of small hotels.

For many years, the bottom end of the Ramblas near the port was a favourite place for buying and selling sex, but the practice was stamped out in the run-up to the 1992 Olympic Games. The municipality and the Friends of the Ramblas association invested millions of pesetas to renovate the area.

LOVE HOTELS

Offering rooms by the hour, love hotels, like those in Japan, are meant for couples. Many of those in Barcelona are designer-built and they are all decorated to satisfy their clients' fantasies: round beds, ceiling mirror, pornographic TV channels, jacuzzis &

La França is one of the biggest and best known, with over seventy luxurious rooms, and it provides private parking, even going so far as covering vehicle license plates to ensure complete discretion.

In the very heart of Barcelona, in El Raval area, La Paloma is a modern hotel for a younger age-group, offering more reasonable tarifs.

The Regàs hotel in Gràcia runs a similar service.

At these three hotels, and generally speaking, at all the love hotels, once you have left the room you cannot return, and there is no need to book in advance. Homosexual couples are welcome, but three in a bed is strictly taboo.

La França.
La França Xica, 40; Tel: 93 423 1416; www.lafransa.com

Regàs
Regàs, 10–12; Tel: 93 238 0092; www.hregas.com

La Paloma
La Paloma, 24–26; Tel: 93 412 4381; www.hlapaloma.com

MUSEU SALVADOR SERRA

La Rambla, 38, 4th floor
Metro: Liceu
• Tel: 93 318 1300

*Private
museum of
photography*

On the fourth floor of No. 38 La Rambla is a very discreet photography museum, known to just a handful of students, professionals, and keen amateur photographers. In its 70 m² are displayed over 3,000 cameras of all types, sizes, and vintages, not to mention those kept in an adjacent storeroom.

Although Salvador Serra was a collector who loved photography, he was never a professional photographer. He was happy taking pictures of his family and his various social acquaintances, and set up a photography shop which today occupies the other four floors of the building. Over time, it has grown to be the largest of its kind in Barcelona.

Mindful of the treasures bequeathed to them by Serra, his heirs decided to temporarily close the museum while seeking more suitable premises, so that the exhibits would not deteriorate.

Among the collectors' items to be found here are bellows cameras dating from 1891, as well as spy cameras from the 1930s to the 1970s.

The technology used to disguise these devices seems somewhat ludicrous today.

A number of Hasselblads are also on display and the history of the Polaroid is documented, along with that of reflex, stereoscopic, and submarine cameras, some of them from Jacques Cousteau's oceanographic ship, *Calypso*.

SIGHTS NEARBY

PIPE COLLECTION AND "SLOW SMOKE" CHAMPIONSHIP

Plaça Reial, 3 principal
Metro: Jaume I
• Tel: 93 302 4732
• Daily, from 18.00
• www.bpipaclub.com

This club-bar dedicated to smoking and tobacco offers a lovely view over the Plaça Reial. The games room (with snooker tables, etc.) has a large collection of pipes and snuff boxes. It also has a workshop to restore the former glory of pipes worn down by old age or ill use.

Among the activities organized by the club, open to the public, is a course on learning to smoke a pipe. Monthly competitions are also held such as the "slow smoke," which involves lighting a pipe filled with 3 grams of tobacco. Whoever keeps the pipe alight longest is declared the winner. The world record is held by an Italian, at 3 hours 48 minutes.

FESTA DELS
CONDUCTORS
Diada de Sant Cristòfol

Mutual de Conductors
Catalana Motor Club Ahora

B · 77807

CAR BLESSING, CAPELLA DE SANT CRISTÒFOR DEL REGOMIR

Carrer Regomir s/n
Metro: Jaume I
• Fridays, 19.00–20.00
• Car blessing: 10 July

> **Blessed be your car …**

Each year on 10 July, all of the taxis in Barcelona queue up to have their vehicle blessed at this tiny chapel built in 1503. The chapel, dedicated to Saint Christopher, patron of travellers in general and taxi drivers in particular, was the first in the country to bless vehicles.

The drivers recall that during the 1970s, when the number of motorists in the city increased dramatically, as many as 2,000 vehicles could be seen waiting their turn for the blessing.

The tradition goes back to 1906, when Cristofol Sarrias, a pharmacist in Carrer de Regomir, and his friend Carles Bonet introduced the French custom of blessing vehicles on St. Christopher's feast day. Only four cars were present at the first ceremony, one of them belonging to the artist Ramón Casas and another to the writer and painter Santiago Rusiñol.

Holding at most twenty people, Saint Christopher's chapel is so small (only two rows of chairs) that the font is outside the building in order not to hinder the flow of worshippers.

Nearby, at the junction of Carrer de Montcada and Carrer dels Carders, is the equally small 12th-century Marcus chapel, named after the philanthropist Bernat Marcus who built a hospital specializing in the treatment of travellers and pilgrims.

SAINT CHRISTOPHER, PROTECTOR OF TRAVELLERS

Reprobus was tall, blond and strong. As an adventurer he sought glory and made up his mind to serve a great king.

He defended the Romans and fought against the Persians until a hermit told him about Jesus, the most powerful of all kings.

Once in the service of Christ, he helped the weak and the ill to cross a dangerous river, until one day there arrived a particularly heavy child. The water was running fast and the child on his back grew heavier and heavier. When the man managed to reach the opposite bank, the Christ child revealed who He was.

From then on the man took the name *Christophorus* ("Christ-Bearer").

Saint Christopher died a martyr, beheaded. Needless to say, he was adopted as the patron saint of travellers.

One of his arms is preserved at Santiago de Compostela and part of his jaw at Astorga (Spain).

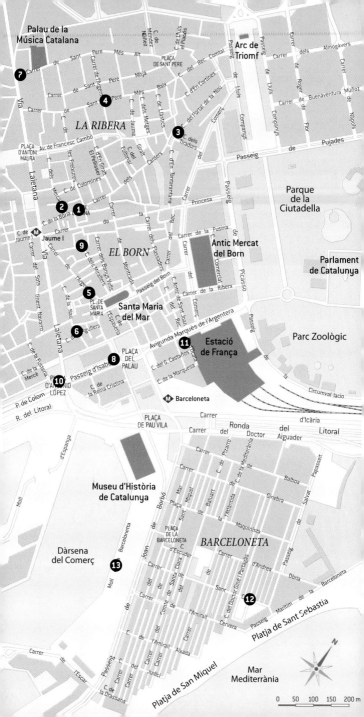

EL BORN - BARCELONETA

LA CUNA DE ORO

Plaça de la Lana, 6
Metro: Jaume I
• Tel: 93 310 1207
• Open Monday to Saturday, 10.00–13.00
and 16.00–20.30

The fortune-teller's world

Opened thirty-five years ago, La Cuna de Oro (The Golden Crib) looks as if it has been frozen in time. At first, the El Born premises specialized in children's clothes and accessories, and business thrived. But after several years, the owner, Mayma, decided to change track and began reading tarot cards, although keeping the original shop's name.

Since then, her establishment serves not only clients of all ages and walks of life seeking a glimpse of their future, but also friends and neighbours in need of a good listener or a shoulder to cry on.

The most striking feature of La Cuna de Oro is the decoration. Every corner is crammed with assorted objects and souvenirs, almost all provided by friends and clients, ranging from photographs and press cuttings to ashtrays, candles, figurines, and thousands of trinkets of purely sentimental value. In this kitsch and cluttered space, Mayma deals with the most diverse subjects, which may be anything from football to culture, local gossip, or esotericism.

While some of her clients have blind faith in her fortune-telling skills, others visit simply to enjoy this unusual and enchanted little place in the heart of Barcelona.

SIGHTS NEARBY
THE MAGIC MUSEUM
Oli, 6
Metro: Jaume I
• Tel: 93 319 7393
• Open Monday to Saturday, 11.00–14.00 and 17.00–20.00

Hidden inside the Rey de la Magia (King of Magic) shop is a small museum, launched in 2002 by two renowned magicians: José María Martínez and Rosa María Llop. They are also the owners of the shop at 11 Calle Princesa, which has been selling magic accessories for the last 125 years.

The museum displays devices used by well-known conjurers and illusionists at different periods, offering a good understanding of the history of magic in Catalonia. These include magic boxes dating from the 1920s, handkerchiefs, magic dice, and eye-catching costumes worn by magicians and their assistants. Unless she is busy planning her next function, the genial Rosa María will give you a guided tour of the museum, stopping to explain "house treasures" such as a picture of magician Carlos Buchel, made from breadcrumbs by a detainee of the Modelo prison. The museum, dedicated to the memory of Fructuoso Canonge (a Plaça Reial shoeshine boy who gained international fame as an illusionist), puts on regular shows and offers six-week courses on escapology techniques and other tricks to amaze your friends.

LLEÓ DEL GREMI DELS PELLAIRES

QUE ES CONSERVÀ FINS L'ANY 1990
EN LES RESTES DE LA CASA GREMIAL
DEL CARRER DELS PETONS.

JOAN AMADES.

THE SYMBOL OF THE FURRIER'S GUILD
Carrer de Portal Nou, 2

*A menacing
lion*

At No. 2 Carrer de Portal Nou, one sees a carved stone lion in a menacing stance. For many years, this was the symbol used by the guild of city furriers.

This association dates back to 1296, and until recently, large earthenware jars also stood here, in which leather was tanned and dyed.

The artisans probably chose this spot because of its plentiful water supply, essential for their daily work.

The Rec Comtal stream ran nearby, supplying the wash-houses of Carrers de Basses de Sant Pere and Tantarantana.

WATER SUPPLY IN OLD BARCELONA

In the same way that many crafts and guilds gave their name to the streets in which they were located (see p. 32), other streets took their names from the emerging industries in a constantly growing city.

One example is Carrer de Basses de Sant Pere, whose name originates from the falls on the Rec Comtal canal which provided power for the city's mills until 1870. The canal also supplied Barcelona with water (the Rec Comtal has given its name to another city street).

It was originally a natural stream, but was later redirected towards the sea. The first reference to the Rec Comtal dates from the year 992, when it was being used to irrigate agricultural areas.

Many medieval guilds located near the canal as an easy means of cleaning their products. Over the years, its waters became increasingly polluted, despite a 1332 law prohibiting disposal of various types of waste, including the remains of animals from the abattoirs.

The canal contributed to the spread of epidemics and to flooding in the city, before it was finally diverted underground in 1801.

SIGHTS NEARBY
BUILDING WITH A LOVE THEME
Carrer de Sant Pere Mes Baix, 46

The main façade of this curious 18th-century building is covered in white figures all relating to different aspects of love. A pair of cupids can also be seen above some of the faces of the men and women represented.

LA PELU

5

Carrer d'Argentería, 70–72
• Metro: Jaime I
• Tel: 93 310 4807

*Hairdresser
of the full moon*

Since the days of grease and hairspray, La Pelu has been dressing and trimming Barcelona's most trendy heads. For the past twenty-seven years it has matched clients' hairdos with their body image, which is no easy task.

It has adapted to changing fashions and gambled on styles that have turned into trendsetters, copied by other hairdressers. La Pelu also offers extra services ranging from stimulating massages and talks to exhibitions of art, jewellery, and other objects, so that clients feel they have done more than spend a few hours at the salon.

The main highlight, however, is the night of the full moon. Once a month, La Pelu stays open all night, turns up the music, and treats clients to free drinks. They queue up in order to have their hair cut at this particular time. Apparently, hair that is cut during a full moon will grow back healthier and stronger than ever …

If you enjoy this experience, there is a similar hairdresser in Paris – details in the guide to *Unusual Shopping in Paris* from this publisher.

FULL MOON LEGENDS

Many popular beliefs associate certain events with the night of the full moon: hair grows faster, criminals feel compelled to gratify their basic instincts (people with mental illnesses find their problems get worse), and suicidal tendencies are aggravated.

It is also claimed that a greater number of women give birth on the night of the full moon (although no scientific study has confirmed this theory), and certain gardening jobs, such as mowing the lawn, benefit from moonlight.

This is plausible because the moon gives off a considerable amount of luminous energy.

Some gardeners and farmers even sow their crops only when the moon is waxing or waning …

Surfaces exposed to moonlight are also thought to become shinier.

celler
Macondo

Areblzzas

Aureliano Buendía

EL CELLER DE MACONDO

Carrer de Consellers, 4

Metro: Jaume I
- Tel: 93 319 4372
- Open Monday to Saturday, 19.00–01.00
- Price per person from €10–€20

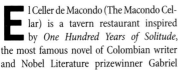

> **A tavern inspired by Garcia Marquez**

El Celler de Macondo (The Macondo Cellar) is a tavern restaurant inspired by *One Hundred Years of Solitude*, the most famous novel of Colombian writer and Nobel Literature prizewinner Gabriel García Márquez. Arnulfo Aldana, owner and fellow Colombian, decides on the musical selection that gives this corner of El Born a Caribbean flavour.

Arnulfo is not only a perfect host, but also an excellent storyteller. His favourite tale is the scandal generated by the name of his restaurant.

When El Celler de Macondo opened its doors ten years ago, the Barcelona representatives of García Márquez sued him for using the name of the village featured in the book.

The story caused a stir, but when García Marquez finally heard about it, he decided to drop the case.

In the end, Arnulfo kept the name, along with the dream that some day the Colombian writer will visit. Main dishes on the menu include the Aureliano Buendía are-pizzas, made from cornflour; the *Variado de Remedios*, which include a sample of Colombian products such as *patacones* (fried plantain) and *buñuelos* (fritters), or the Macondesa salad in which ingredients from the five continents can be found. Arnulfo also offers his *Melquíades* meat pies and *Úrsula* desserts, as well as various recipes that he learned in different ports in his merchant seaman days.

SIGHTS NEARBY

CASA DEL GREMIO MUSICAL
Carrer de Sant Pere Alto, 1

This building, dating from 1763, was once the meeting place for members of the musical guild. The façade features a medallion and magnificent frescoes engraved in the stone, beneath a garland of cherubs.

FREEMASON SYMBOLS AT 7 PORTES RESTAURANT

⑧

Passeig Isabel II, 14

Metro: Barceloneta
- Tel: 93 319 3033
- Open daily from 13.00 to 01.00
- Price per person: approx. €30 – €50

> **A restaurant modelled on King Solomon's Temple**

F ew of its many customers are aware of the secrets and anecdotes hidden behind the doors of this emblematic restaurant. The building is said to have been modelled on the Temple of King Solomon, and together with its ground-floor restaurant, it is full of freemasonry symbols.

The signs of the zodiac engraved in the columns and the classic freemason triangle leave little room for doubt. Looking up, you can see the image of the Greek god Cronus (Saturn to the Romans), the lord of the titans, and each entrance is headed by the restaurant's name written in different alphabets.

This restaurant, open since 1836, was for many years the meeting place for secret Masonic fraternities, hence all the symbolism. The interior is also worth a closer look, with a chequered floor, characteristic of Masonic lodges, and an acacia branch, a tree that freemasons consider sacred.

Among other historic curiosities, it is notable that this was the first building in Barcelona to have running water. Also, the very first photograph to be taken in Spain was of its façade. In fact, the restaurant is on the ground floor of one of the city's most memorable buildings, Porxos d'en Xifré, constructed in the 1830s.

The man behind this building was Josep Xifré y Cases (1777–1856), a Spaniard who had made his fortune in Cuba by exporting sugar from the slave plantations to the United States.

Xifré later travelled to New York, where he multiplied his wealth. In 1831, he returned to Barcelona, investing his money in banking and real estate. The building and the arcades that surround the restaurant, which pay homage to his life, were designed by Josep Buixareu and Francesc Vila.

Above the main entrance is the following inscription: "Uranus observes the movement of the sky and the stars," and there are also medallions portraying the great explorers and conquistadors that Xifré tried to emulate: Columbus, Pizarro, Magellan, and Cortés. Between the arches, a number of sculpted trophies evoke his "success" in the Americas, including a cornucopia overflowing with gold coins, a chest filled with accounting books, and a slave's head.

EROTIC SCULPTURES IN MIRALLERS STREET
Metro: Jaume I

Ecstatic expressions

Located in Barcelona's old quarter, between the Barrio Gótico and El Born neighbourhoods, above the northern corner of Carrer dels Mirallers, a woman's head is carved in the stone. Her eyes are blank and she seems terrified, but a closer look reveals that her expression is actually one of intense pleasure. In fact, this face, which blends in discreetly with the façade, indicated to passers-by the presence of a brothel in the vicinity.

Barcelona's port used to receive hundreds of sailors and foreigners who, once ashore, would set out in search of these so-called "pleasure houses." Stone representations like this one were perfect signposts, both for foreigners and for those who could not read.

In the 1400s, certain brothels were tolerated and protected by the government. In fact, in 1452, King Alfonso V of Aragon granted Simón Sala a special permit so that he could open a string of brothels around town. However, during Holy Week the prostitutes had to remain behind closed doors and not display their bodies, to avoid tempting the faithful to sin.

SIGHTS NEARBY
MURALS AT THE POST OFFICE BUILDING
Plaça d'Antonio López s/n

The ceiling of the great circular lobby of the Edificio de Correos y Telégrafos has a series of fine paintings dating from the early 20th century, which often go unnoticed by customers.

The most striking among them shows a Roman cart pulled by deer, carrying an old man who is holding in his arms a completely unexpected object – a toy locomotive that seems out of place in this Renaissance-inspired fresco. It is of course an allegory, devised by the visionary painter Francesc Canyellas i Balaguero (Barcelona, 1899–1938).

"THE FLOWER OF THE WORLD'S MOST BEAUTIFUL CITIES"

Miguel de Cervantes is believed to have lived in the square where the Post Office building is located. His biographers say that this would have been in 1569 when Cervantes was 22 years old and was fleeing to Italy from Madrid. The author of *Don Quixote* wrote of Barcelona: "Of the world's most beautiful cities, this is the flower."

FRIENDS OF THE RAILWAY ASSOCIATION

Estació de França (south entrance)
Carrer d'Ocata s/n
• Metro: Barceloneta
• Tel: 93 310 5297
• Open Tuesday, Thursday and Friday 18.00–21.00,
  Saturday 17.00–21.30
• www.aafcb.org

*Miniature
trains*

Founded in 1944, Barcelona's Friends of the Railway Association (*Asociación de Amigos del Ferrocarril de Barcelona*) is a dream come true for rail lovers. Located in the south wing of the França station, it occupies three vast rooms.

One holds the library and has specialized magazines, films, and over 4,000 volumes available to members. Collector's items are found in every available space: signals, telegraph machines, old posters, and hundreds of model trains, replicating both famous and little-known engines.

The second hall is open to members who want to run their model trains and feel like real train drivers. The tracks twist and intersect in such a way that the enthusiastic operators must be on their guard and employ some basic skills to avoid an accident in miniature. Finally, there is a conference hall where lectures and courses are held, and rail films and documentaries projected. The most striking aspect of this room is the seating, both for conference participants and the general public, which comes from authentic rolling stock.

The association, in collaboration with the Renfe/ADIF rail company and the Catalan Government Railways, organizes special outings to discover vintage and modern trains. The AAFCB also has its own collection of vintage trains, such as the *Garrat 106* steam locomotive dating from 1926, the *Berga 31* steam train from 1902 fitted with wooden carriages, and the *Patxanga 304* electric train from 1926. During May, June, July, and August, trips on these trains are organized to nearby villages, where a stop is usually made for lunch, the idea being to recreate the ambience of an earlier age.

The association can be visited without pre-booking if you are just passing through. If you wish to join and participate in their conferences, excursions, or become a model train driver, the inscription fee is €30 and the annual fee €98.

There is a similar organization in Paris, with premises located beneath the Gare de l'Est (see Secret Paris, in the same collection as this guide).

THE HAND OF BARCELONETA
Carrer de Sant Carles, 35 and Carrer de Soria, 18

A mysterious sculpture

To this day there is no known explanation of the origin of the mysterious hand sculpted in stone at the corner of Sant Carles and Soria streets. Located 3 metres above ground level, the palm of the hand faces downwards and incorporates two triangles that indicate opposite directions. Perhaps it was a bricklayer's joke or a stonemason's whim, no one knows for sure. But it has survived over the years and succesive restorations of the building.

The construction of Barceloneta started in 1753 and is the work of the military engineer Juan Martín Cermeño.

At first the houses had only one floor, until 1838, when a second floor could be added. In 1868 a third floor was authorized, and in 1872 a fourth. The house with the hand of Barceloneta dates from 1875.

BARCELONA'S FIRST MAN-MADE DISTRICT

Barceloneta was constructed to provide housing for fishermen and workers displaced by the Ciudadela fortress built after the Bourbon conquest of Barcelona in 1714.

Engineer Cermeño, putting his military skills to use, drew up a perfect grid composed of fifteen narrow streets intersected by five avenues. Cermeño, who later created the Ramblas, launched the modernization of the area, always with a long-term vision, on ground reclaimed from the sea. Only the point of the triangle, Maians island (now concreted over) was previously above water. Because of its location and Barcelona's strong military significance, Barceloneta has always been a strategic point.

SIGHTS NEARBY

THE CLOCK TOWER AND THE DECIMAL METRIC SYSTEM

At the end of the 18th century, the Torre del Rellotge served as one of the reference points for French astronomer Pierre-François Méchain's project to define a decimal metric system based on the Earth's circumference (see p. 126). A plaque from 1999 celebrates the bicentenary of his work. Another point of reference for Méchain was the Fontana de Oro hotel, in Carrer dels Escudellers, where he stayed during his time in Barcelona.

As an homage to the metre, architect Ildefons Cerdá, the man responsible for planning the Eixample district, laid out avenues Paral·lel and Meridiana in a fashion so that if their routes were extended eastwards and southwards, respectively, they would intersect at the clock tower.

EL RAVAL

LA VANGUARDIA

NOTAS GRAFICAS — BARCELONA

Miércoles 28 de Septiembre de 1932

EL JEFE DEL GOBIERNO EN MONTSERRAT

CUATRO PÁ

EN LA PRENSA DE AQUEL DÍA ...

Carrer del Tigre, 20
Metro: Universitat
• Tel: 93 302 5996
• Open Monday to Friday 10.00–13.30 and 17.00–20.00
• www.periodicosregalo.com

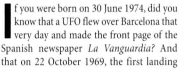

An original gift

I f you were born on 30 June 1974, did you know that a UFO flew over Barcelona that very day and made the front page of the Spanish newspaper *La Vanguardia*? And that on 22 October 1969, the first landing strip in Antarctica was inaugurated? Reading the papers of the last 100 years is addictive. *En la prensa de aquel día ...* ("In the press that day ...") has them all in stock, or almost all, as some dates are so popular that they run out.

This archival service was a natural consequence of the owner wondering how to make use of a vast quantity of old newspapers. She later acquired other titles and the small collection became an important historical archive.

Most of the people who come into the shop want to know what happened on the day of their birth (or that of a loved one), or perhaps the day of their marriage.

So the staff rummage through the stacks of old magazines (vacuum-wrapped to protect them from humidity) until they find the relevant date.

You can choose between just the front page, the complete publication, or even an advertisement.

The shop also sells another original gift: personalized crosswords. All you have to do is supply a few details about the person you want to surprise: date of birth, tastes, habits, good and bad qualities, or whatever else you can think of to form the basis of an entertaining puzzle.

SIGHTS NEARBY

FORMER TAX OFFICES

At No. 54 Carrer de Sant Antoni Abat stands a building that until a century ago was the tax collection centre. These places were generally found on the outskirts of Spanish cities or close to their ports, so that the merchants of the time had to pass them on the way into the city centre.

CARITAT PERLOS
PORRES DEL HOS
PITAL D NOSTRA
SENYORA DELS
YNFANTS
ORFANS

AÑY 1785

ALMS BOX
Carrer d'Elisabets, 24

The wood and metal collection box at No. 24 Carrer d'Elisabets dates from 1785. It stands at the entrance to the Centre d'Informació i Documentació Internacional de Barcelona (CIDOB), formerly a hospice chapel. A Maltese cross is engraved on the box along with the inscription: *Caritat per los pobres del hospital de Nostra Senyora dels Ynfants Orfans* ("Offering for the poor of the hospital of Our Lady of the Orphan Children"). This institution, founded in 1370 by Guillem de Pou, was a hospice for orphaned children aged between 7 and 12. The building, restored by the architect Pau Granados, is in excellent condition. On the adjacent site of a former church (Iglesia de la Misericòrdia) there is now a bookshop, La Central. Inside are two angels holding aloft the city's coat of arms. The Gothic-style building has also kept its vaulted ceilings.

"JAZZ IS THE MUSIC GOD DANCES TO WHEN NOBODY IS LOOKING"
The Catalan novelist, Egyptologist, cinema critic, and essayist Terenci Moix (Barcelona, 1942–2003), was born at No. 37 Carrer de Joaquím Costa. Later, the building was used as a dairy, run by the same couple who have now converted it into a bar for poets. They still have the containers and measuring utensils that used to hold fresh milk for sale.

Today the place is full of charm, and when you go inside it is obvious that TV and gaming machines are banned. You can listen to good jazz or classical music instead. Carlos Julio and Montse, the two owners, are passionate about jazz and, of course, the work of Terenci Moix, who visited his old home a number of times.

Above the bar are the attic rooms where the writer grew up. Many of his fans go up there, as well as poetry lovers. Every fortnight, a poetry reading is held where participants take turns reading extracts from a well-known writer or from their own work.

The poems, reflections, and thoughts of visitors stuck to the tiled walls are one of most interesting features here. Some of these are inspired by music: "Jazz is the music God dances to when nobody is looking," others have a more social message: "If some lived more simply, others would live, simply". Most are anonymous, although a few are signed by cult local poets such as Lola García.

GRANJA DEGAVA
Carrer de Joaquím Costa, 37.
Metro: Sant Antoni
• Tel: 93 317 5883.
• Open Monday to Saturday, 8.00–22.00

SIGHTS NEARBY

HOME CINEMA   ❹

Voidzelig
Carrer de Ferlandina, 51
Metro: Universitat
• Open Tuesday to Sunday, 17.30–23.00
• www.void-bcn.com

Voidzelig is a video club offering the widest selection of independent and director's films in the city.

These films can also be viewed in the club, on a wide screen in a private cinema. Hire of the projection room for two hours (capacity: 30) costs €40.

A SHOP THAT ISN'T A SHOP: GRANJA PUY   ❺

Carrer de la Cera, 7
• Metro: Sant Antoni

Carrer de la Cera, so called because many years ago it was home to a candlemaker, is one of the most picturesque areas of El Raval. In this mixed-race area, at No. 7 is Granja Puy, a place as mysterious as it is unusual.

Although on the surface it looks like a shop filled with bric-a-brac, displaying diverse collector's items in the window such as an old radio, a poster advertising a 1960s brand of yogurt, teacups, and a battered old soft toy, it is in fact a family home.

The lady of the house nevertheless responds to anyone who rings her doorbell asking the price of the radio or the poster.

Although nothing is supposed to be for sale, it sometimes happens, depending on the time of day or the interest shown in the coveted object, that the owner will finally decide to sell. Best not turn up at siesta time though …

THE TORTURED SOULS OF THE SANT ANTONI MARKET

Legend has it that the gallows where certain prisoners were decapitated in the Middle Ages were outside the city walls, on the exact spot where the Sant Antoni market is held today. For years nobody wanted to buy this land, fearful of the stories of ghosts and other paranormal phenomena. Nobody, that is, until 1882, when Antoni Rovira i Trìas, the renowned architect who missed his chance to go down in posterity as the mastermind of the Eixample development (he won the commission, but it was transferred to Ildefons Cerdà by royal decree), inaugurated the Sant Antoni market, one of his major projects.

ANATOMY LECTURE HALL ❻

Real Academia de Medicina
Carrer del Carme, 47
Metro: Liceu
• Tel: 93 317 1686
• Open Wednesday, 10.00–13.00

Barcelona's secret masterpiece of neoclassical architecture

Designed by the surgeon Pere Virgili and built in 1760 by Ventura Rodríguez, the P. Gimbernat anatomy lecture hall of Barcelona's Royal Academy of Medicine and Surgery is a a little-known masterpiece of neoclassical architecture.

This dark and gloomy place has an atmosphere that can be overwhelming, inviting silence and inspiring respect. The circular hall, while not very large, has a very high ceiling. In the centre stands a marble table equipped with a hole to drain away the blood of the bodies being dissected.

Its proximity to the Santa Creu hospital of course made it easier to perform demonstrations on human corpses.

Notable among the operations carried out at the time (1770) was the spectacular separation of Siamese twin boys.

The benches where the students sat surrounded the dissection table. In the front rows were a dozen wooden armchairs reserved for the authorities. A chandelier hangs from the ceiling and between the high windows are busts of a number of immortal figures from Barcelona's medical world, such as Ramón y Cajal, Servet, and Mata.

The building was initially home to the College of Surgery, then until 1904 served as the Faculty of Medicine. It subsequently become a training school and, since 1920, has belonged to the Royal Academy of Medicine. In 1951 it was listed as a historic and artistic monument of national interest.

Once a year, Catalan writers meet in the lecture hall to "dissect" the Catalan language, discuss the changing vocabulary, the future of the language, and additions to the dictionary.

Visiting is very restricted, with public access on Wednesday mornings only. It is no use trying to gain entry at other times.

There is a similar hall in London – see Secret London: An Unusual Guide, in this collection of guidebooks.

EL TORN DELS ORFES

Carrer de les Ramelleres, 17
Metro: Catalunya

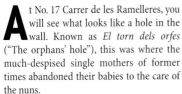

Drop off your children ...

At No. 17 Carrer de les Ramelleres, you will see what looks like a hole in the wall. Known as *El torn dels orfes* ("The orphans' hole"), this was where the much-despised single mothers of former times abandoned their babies to the care of the nuns.

The Casa de la Misericòrdia, founded in 1583 at Plaça de Vicenç Martorell, 300 years later became the *Casa Provincial de Maternidad y Expósitos* (Provincial Home for Expectant Mothers and Waifs).

The hole, a sort of pivoting window into which the babies were placed, was in service from the mid-19th century to 1931. The building has since been renovated and converted into the administrative headquarters of the Ciutat Vella district. The hole, however, has been preserved as being of historical significance.

THE WHEEL OF THE INNOCENTS

As early as 787, a Milanese priest named Dateo is said to have placed a shell outside his church to collect abandoned babies.

From 1188, the first initiatives to save such infants were organized at Chanoines hospice in Marseille (France), before Pope Innocent III (1160–1216, pontiff from 1198 until his death) institutionalized the practice.

Witnessing the terrible spectacle of the bodies of abandoned children floating on the Tiber in Rome, he planned a way to save them.

Installed at the doors of convents and designed to preserve the anonymity of desperate parents, the "wheel of the innocents" consisted of a revolving crib accessible from the outside.

The baby was placed in the crib and a bell rung to warn the sisters who would then turn the wheel to bring it inside the convent.

Note that access to the wheel was protected by a calibrated grille that would only allow newborn babies to pass through ... This system was dropped in the 19th century but after a couple of decades had to be resurrected throughout Europe as the practice of abandoning children again became widespread.

SIGHTS NEARBY

STATUE OF SAINT ROCH   ❽

In the patio of the former Santa Creu hospital stands a sculpture of Saint Roch, protector and healer of plague victims, accompanied by a dog and a child.

The saint seems to be lifting his robe in an ambivalent gesture. In fact, he is revealing the scars that the disease had left on his thigh, the part of the body where plague symptoms tend to appear first. During the 15th century, the quest to ward off infectious diseases increased the popularity of holy figures such as Saint Roch.

WATER CISTERN, INSTITUTO DE ESTUDIOS CATALANES   ❾

The Institute of Catalan Studies, a short distance from the Royal Academy of Medicine, occupies part of the former Santa Creu hospital, which was founded in 1401. In the central patio and surrounded by magnificent columns and mosaics, the statue of Saint Paul by Lluís Bonifaç (1696) conceals a secret: if you look under one of the supporting pillars you will see a very deep well. The patio has been built over a vast water cistern. Ask permission from the concierge if you want to visit.

RAMÓN Y CAJAL'S HOUSE   ❿
Carrer del Notariat, 7; Metro: Liceu

At No. 7 Carrer del Notariat, a plaque records that in this building the joint winner of the Nobel Prize for Physiology or Medicine in 1906, Santiago Ramón y Cajal (1852–1934), developed his "theory of the neurone," a decisive stage in understanding the structure of the nervous system. Ramón y Cajal also studied sculpture, worked as an apprentice shoemaker, and was a keen photographer.

Beginning in his youth, when he stole two corpses to study anatomy in a barn, he showed his innate talent for furthering knowledge of the human body. A specialist in histology and a pioneer in neurology, his publications and discoveries took the scientific world by surprise. As Nobel laureate he travelled the world to disseminate his work.

EL RAVAL

In Roman times, El Raval ("the hamlet"), from the Arab word *rabid*, was a region of fields, orchards, and marshland.

From the Roman town, Barcino, three routes crossed it: one that led to Llobregat (now Carrer del Hospital), one that led to Sarrià (Carrer dels Tallers), and the Montjuic road.

The city began to expand along these access roads, first merging with the monasteries, leper homes, and hospitals, then taking in the market towns of the surrounding countryside.

PETRAS

Mercat de la Boquería • Plaça de la Boquería • Stalls 866–870
Metro: Liceu • Tel: 93 302 5273
• Open Monday to Saturday, 8.00–14.00

AVINOVA

Mercat de la Boquería • Aisle 1, stalls 703–707
• Tel: 93 301 3071 • Open Monday to Saturday, 8.00–20.30

Ants, scorpions and kangaroos on the menu

Although bats are eaten in Thailand and chicken embryos in the Philippines, in Barcelona you can sample ants, worms, crickets, and a vast range of crunchy, tasty insects at very reasonable prices.

A dozen large ants imported from Colombia, ideal for an aperitif, can cost up to €3 at Petras, which occupies stalls 866–870 of La Boquería market.

A tin of worms, which are to Thailand what chips are to Europe, is €4 to €5.

If savoury snacks do nothing for your taste buds, there are also scorpion lollies.

Insects are nearly always prepared the same way: fried until crisp in a large quantity of oil.

If you're looking for more exotic ingredients, another stallholder, Avinova (aisle 1, stalls 703–707) offers reindeer meat imported from Sweden (€61 per kilo), or a woodpigeon to roast for the family Sunday lunch, not to mention pheasant, partridge, hare, kangaroo, and coming soon, turtle fillets for the most adventurous.

SIGHTS NEARBY

MUSEO DEL WHISKY

Carrer de les Sitges, 3
• Metro: Catalunya
• Tel: 93 318 5145

At the Scotch Tavern and Museo del Whisky not only can you sample the beverage, but also listen to 1980s music in the company of a very strange selection of nocturnal revellers. The museum boasts a collection of 600 brands of whisky, the centrepiece being a 1946 bottle of The Macallan. Only 246 bottles of this vintage were produced, of which Spain imported twenty, three going to Barcelona and one to this bar. Its price of 1,000,000 pesetas was slightly more than the going rate of €6,000. As devoted fans of the liquid for which the bar is named, the waiters are not very reliable: it is difficult to find out what day or what time the bar opens.

HORA OFICIAL

REIAL ACADÈMIA DE CIÈNCIES

REIAL ACADÈMIA DE CIÈNCIES I ARTS LIBRARY ⑬

La Rambla, 155; Metro: Catalunya; Tel: 93 317 0536
- In winter, open Monday to Thursday, 16.00–19.00
- In summer, Monday to Thursday, 10.00–13.00
- Guided tours offered on some summer Saturdays
- www.racab.es

City time

The façade of the library of the Royal Academy of Sciences and Arts of Barcelona features a clock constructed in 1869 and designated in 1891 as the official municipal timepiece.

In theory, tours of the interior of this Art Nouveau building, designed by the architect Josep Doménech i Estapà and inaugurated in 1894, are restricted. However, the authorities organize occasional guided tours on Saturdays. Otherwise, you may be admitted as a researcher, a university member or out of simple curiosity to see its fabulous collection of antique clocks.

The library archives contain over 150,000 volumes on pure and applied science. Many of them were judged by the Inquisition as likely to damage religious sensitivities and placed on the Roman Catholic Church's Index of Forbidden Books in 1773.

On the second floor of the building are the meeting rooms and an exhibition space given over to scientific instruments, collectors' items such as a 16th-century astrolabe and the antique clocks. The most remarkable of these is an astronomical clock that gives the hour and the rising and setting times of the sun in twenty-four capital cities, and is equipped with a perpetual calendar and planetary drive bearing the signs of the zodiac. This masterpiece of clock-making is by Albert Billeter, designer of the Gràcia clock tower.

THE RAMBLAS

The promenade known as the Ramblas is an invention of Barcelona whose name derives from the Arab word *ramlah* (sandbank).
Elsewhere in Spain, a *rambla* is a natural runoff for heavy rainwater. In Catalonia, it has come to signifie a tree-lined avenue with sidewalks and a broad central strip given over to stalls and kiosks among which the crowds stroll.

LOVE IN A HELICOPTER

Bagdad, Tel: 93 442 0777; www.bagdad.com
Bagdad is Barcelona's most well-known cabaret, largely because it was the first place in the country to legally offer a pornographic show. The establishment also pioneered in organizing entertainment on board a helicopter or an aerostatic balloon. But for the more conventional clients or those afraid of heights, Bagdad has limousines for hire in the company of congenial young men or women...

HAND OF GOD, SANT PAU DEL CAMP MONASTERY

⑭

Carrer de Sant Pau, 101
Metro: Paral-lel
• Open Monday to Friday, 16.00–20.00;
Saturday, 10.00–14.00 and 16.00–20.00
• Admission: €2

> *The hand of God as a symbol of power ...*

Sant Pau del Camp monastery, listed as a national heritage in 1879, originally stood outside the city walls in the countryside.

Despite having been absorbed by the modern city centre, it retains some of its bucolic charm. It must have been built before 911, although there is no proof of the exact date other than the tomb of the man who commissioned it, Count Guifré-Borrell.

On the façade above the main doorway, a hand with two outstretched fingers can be seen carved in a circular niche, together with an angel and an eagle, both heavily eroded with the passage of time. The image is repeated inside the church, beneath a bench.

This Christian symbol of the hand of God was often used in the Middle Ages to represent divine power.

It is always the right hand, the strongest hand, generally depicted in large format to illustrate the colossal power of God acting through the Church. Although here the hand is making a sign of benediction, it is sometimes found in a commanding or threatening gesture.

The origin of this symbol lies in the Hebrew word iad, meaning both hand and power.

The cloister is the most important part of the monastery from an architectural point of view.

It has four entrances surmounted by trefle arches, posed on columns whose capitals are decorated with animal and plant motifs.

Throughout its history, the monastery has undergone successive devastation and renovation.

During the Napoleonic occupation between 1808 and 1814, it also became a hospital for French troops, then a garrison for Italian soldiers. In 1814, thanks to Professor Joan de Zafont, it was reopened as a centre of religious teaching.

THE FLOODS OF 1981

On 21 August 1981, torrential rain battered Barcelona and flooded the monastery to a depth of 2 metres. A notice on one of the doors recounts the events of that day.

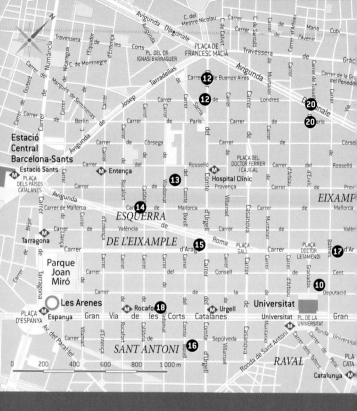

EIXAMPLE

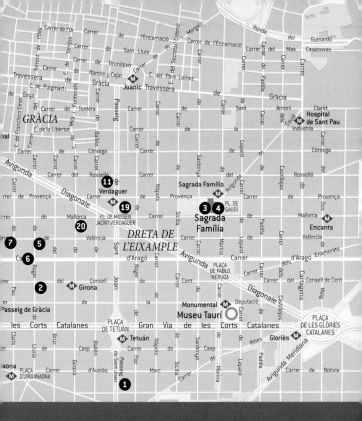

BIBLIOTECA PÚBLICA ARÚS

①

Passeig de Sant Joan, 26 principal
Metro: Arc de Triomf
- Tel: 93 232 5404
- Open Monday to Thursday, 10.00–14.00 and
  15.00–19.00 and Friday, 9.00–14.30
- www.bpa.es
- Reader's card: €20, renewable every three years
- Free admission for students

Everything
you always
wanted to know
about ...

Everything about the Arús Library is distinctive – from the luminous and pleasant entrance to the coloured marble staircase and the word "Salve" engraved there to greet visitors. No specific style defines the place. The first impression, however, is a mysterious lack of proportion, with the rooms and their objects somehow seeming either too large or too small.

Before it was made a library, this was the private residence of Rossend Arús, a philanthropist, playwright, and masonic Grand Master, who believed that the only path to redemption was through knowledge. He died young (1847–1891) and his great legacy was this eccentric home with its extensive library on freemasonry, anarchy, and contemporary social movements.

All his life Arús thoroughly documented what was happening around him in notebooks that can be consulted in the library. The writings show his attempts to free freemasonry from any religious influence and to abandon the rituals that linked the masons with esotericism.

Founded in 1895, the library is crammed with curious details. At the top of the central staircase hangs a commemorative plaque in recognition of Arús' masonic work as Grand Master of the Regional Symbolic Grand Lodge.

Next to the plaque are Ionic columns and decorative borders painted with ancient Greek patterns, leading to a 2-metre replica of the Statue of Liberty, further underlining Arús' belief that the path to freedom is through enlightenment.

Arús himself is depicted in a portrait prominently displayed in the library, and by a bust near the exit.

The heir to a family fortune, he was bald, sported a moustache and was very elegant in his frockcoat.

He also wrote several plays. Visitors to the library can benefit from this inspiring place with its memories of Aeschylus, Poe and the other great authors he admired.

GARDENS OF TORRE DE LAS AGUAS

Carrer de Roger de Llúria, 56
Metro: Girona
- January, February, November and December, open 10.00–18.00
- March and October, 10.00–19.00
- April and September, 10.00–20.00
- May, June, July and August, 10.00–21.00

**An oasis
in the city**

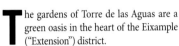

The gardens of Torre de las Aguas are a green oasis in the heart of the Eixample ("Extension") district.

A wrought-iron gate, designed by Robert Llimós and decorated with undulating waves, welcomes visitors into this relaxing place.

The idea of setting such havens of peace amidst residential blocks originated with Ildefons Cerdà, the engineer who masterminded the Eixample expansion.

In fact, the gardens of Torre de las Aguas are one of the few places that survived intact from his original plans.

The magnificent and imposing tower formerly provided the neighbourhood with water, hence its name, and it is still a meeting point for local residents. Erected by architect Josep Oriol Mestres and engineer Antoní Darder in 1870, the tower presides over a small pool that is very popular with children in summer.

MASONIC EIXAMPLE?

Until 1859, Barcelona was surrounded by city walls, but at the beginning of the 19th century the city had begun to expand beyond these confines. The engineer responsible for urbanizing the zone between the old city centre of Barcelona and the Collserola hills behind was Ildefons Cerdà, a forward-thinking man also thought to be a freemason, although there is no conclusive evidence to prove his affiliation to the lodges.

The grid of the Eixample, that extends the area between Avinguda Diagonal, Plaça de Espanya and Avinguda Carlos I, is composed of perfectly marked-out squares. Some believe that this obsession with squares in Cerdà's designs must be a masonic influence. Whether this is true or not, his mission was to make the Eixample an egalitarian district, where differences would be obliterated and there would be no obvious centre of power, endowed with plentiful green spaces and recreational land for the residents to enjoy. The intention behind his urban plan was to stop the city from being a breeding-ground for disease, and ensure that the Eixample would be a light-filled area with patio gardens, trees, wide streets, and low-rise buildings, all rather similar in style, to give a sense of social equality. However, most of the ideas behind his project were not put into practice, as over time the real-estate developers disregarded many of its provisions on building heights and densities.

EXPIATORY TEMPLE OF THE HOLY FAMILY ❸

Carrer de Mallorca, 401
Metro: Sagrada Família
- Tel: 93 207 3031
- Open from October to March, 9.00–18.00;
  April to September, 9.00–20.00
- Closed afternoons of 25 and 26 December and 1–6 January
- Admission: €8
- www.sagradafamilia.org

Mystery of the magic square

The magic square is one of the greatest mysteries behind Gaudí's unfinished masterpiece, the Temple Expiatori de la Sagrada Família.

Its grid is made up of a series of numbers, the sum of which is always 33 whether they are totalled horizontally, vertically or diagonally.

Generally in this type of grid, the result tends to be 34, not 33. The square, like the other sculptures in the atrium, are not Gaudí's own work but that of Josep María Subirachs, the sculptor who made the church his home for seventeen years (1987–2004) in order to carry out his own ambitious artistic project. Subirachs' magic square, which is in the porch next to the Kiss of Judas, together with a series of statues representing various scenes from the life of Christ, has inspired many interpretations.

The first theory links it to Christ, who died at the age of 33.

The second explanation relates the grid to the masonic lodges because 33 corresponds to the number of grades (degrees of initiation) that a freemason can acquire.

The number is derived from giving the Greek capital letter gamma a value of 3, and lambda the value of 30. The characteristic symbols of the lodges are the set square, represented by gamma, and the compass, represented by lambda: total 33.

Subirachs, with his magic square, may have wanted to hint at Gaudí's supposed masonic affiliation, although this has never actually been confirmed. Furthermore, Gaudí's life was so geared towards work and religion that few believe he even had the time to become a member of any kind of masonic lodge.

A third explanation of the square holds that it is a tribute to Albrecht Dürer and his engraving Melancolia, which dates from 1514.

This picture also has a magic square, but its numbers add up to 34.

SIGHTS NEARBY

SAGRADA FAMÍLIA LABYRINTH

On the Passion façade (Carrer de Sardenya, facing west) is a labyrinth sculpted in stone, next to which is a serpent whose tail is said to symbolize personal fulfilment. The façade, also by Subirachs, has only recently been completed. In theory, it respects Gaudí's initial project, although it is difficult to be certain to what extent, because his original plans, models and sketches were destroyed during the Civil War. On the other hand, Subirachs' work has caused great controversy as it bears little relation to Gaudí's realist style.

LABYRINTHS AND THEIR SYMBOLISM

In Greek mythology, one of the first labyrinths was built by Dædalus to enclose the Minotaur, a creature born of the love between Queen Pasiphæ, the wife of King Minos of Crete, and a bull. According to some archæologists, the origin of this myth may lie in the complex plans of the Palace of Minos in Knossos, Crete. Only three people were able to find their way out of the maze: the first was Theseus, who had gone to Crete to kill the beast. Ariadne, daughter of Minos, fell in love with Theseus and gave him a ball of thread so that he could find his way out. Dædalus was also able to escape along with his son Icarus after he was imprisoned in his own labyrinth by Minos. (Some versions say that Minos wanted to prevent Dædalus revealing the plans to this labyrinth, others that Minos wanted to punish him for giving Ariadne the idea of the thread.) It turned out that Dædalus' own design for the labyrinth was so cunning that the only way for him to escape was to fly out using the wings he had made for himself and Icarus from feathers and wax.

Although the Mesopotamian, Egyptian, Hopi, and Navaho civilisations all designed and built labyrinths, there are also examples located in Europe dating from prehistory. Other notable labyrinths built in the Christian era are to be found in the catacombs of Rome and in the churches of San Michele Maggiore in Pavia, San Savino in Plasencia, and in Lucca (Italy), as well as at Chartres and Reims (France).

These labyrinths tend to face westwards, the direction that evil spirits are said to come from (the west, where the sun sets, represents death). As these evil spirits are believed to advance in a straight line, the labyrinths are designed to trap them before they reach the churches' choir.

The relatively complex symbolism of labyrinths is also linked to the meaning of life, signifying man wandering through the universe, ignorant of where he is coming from or where he is going. At the same time, the centre of the labyrinth represents the safe haven of divine salvation and the heavenly Jerusalem — reached only after a necessary rite of passage that may be painful and tortuous at times. The attainment of this goal is symbolized by the flight of Dædalus and Icarus, which denotes both the elevation of the spirit towards knowledge and of the soul towards God. Ariadne's love for Theseus symbolizes love for another being, the two halves that permit an escape from the absurd human condition.

DELICATESSEN QUEVIURES MÚRRIA

Carrer de Roger de Llúria, 85
Metro: Passeig de Gràcia
- Tel: 93 215 5789
- Open Monday to Friday, 9.00–14.00
  and 17.00–21.00

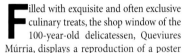

*Darwin's
monkey*

Filled with exquisite and often exclusive culinary treats, the shop window of the 100-year-old delicatessen, Queviures Múrria, displays a reproduction of a poster designed by Ramón Casas, a Modernist painter who was well known in Barcelona for his graphic designs. This poster was commissioned for the liquor *Anís del Mono* (The Monkey's Anise) and although it is not the original picture, which is in the private collection of the Osborne family, it is valuable none the less.

In 1898, Ramón Casas won a competition sponsored by the BBosch distilleries in Barcelona.

The winner would go down in history by immortalizing the Anís del Mono logo. Casas found his inspiration from the stir caused by Darwin with *On the Origin of Species*, published in 1859. He interpreted Darwin's theory – that man is descended from the ape – in a rather haphazard but effective manner, and wrote on the label: "It's the best. Science says so and I don't lie." Casas won the competition, and *Anís del Mono* became an unprecedented success, which other liquor brands have tried in vain to emulate.

> Queviures Múrria is a legendary store. It opened in 1898 as a coffee roaster and biscuit factory. In those days it was called La Purísima, taking its name from a nearby church.

SIGHTS NEARBY

THE CHURCH THAT CHANGED ITS NEIGHBOURHOOD

Iglesia de la Concepción
Aragó, 295. Metro: Girona • Tel: 93 457 6552
- Open Monday to Sunday, 8.00–13.00 and 17.00–21.00

The Church of the Conception has not always stood at No. 295 Carrer d'Aragó. It used to be in Carrer de Jonqueres, but was dismantled brick by brick in 1869 and transferred to its new home. The move and reconstruction, supervised by Jeroni Granelli i Mundet, began on 29 June and took two years to complete.

Originally built in the 14th century, this Gothic church had formed part of the monastery of Jonqueres, until the municipality reclaimed the plot of land for urban development. The parishioners succeeded in having the church moved onto unbuilt land with only trees and meadows at the time, but which later became part of the Eixample). In 1879, a bell tower was added from the San Miguel church, which had also been demolished.

NOCTURNAL VISITS TO THE EGYPTIAN MUSEUM

Carrer de València, 284
- Tel: 93 488 0188
- Open Monday to Saturday, 10.00–20.00 and Sunday, 10.00–14.00
- Admission: €7
- www.fundclos.com
- Dramatized nocturnal visits: Friday and Saturday (except public holidays) at 21.30:
- €20 per person
- Egyptian banquet: €30

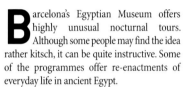

A dinner fit for a pharaoh

Barcelona's Egyptian Museum offers highly unusual nocturnal tours. Although some people may find the idea rather kitsch, it can be quite instructive. Some of the programmes offer re-enactments of everyday life in ancient Egypt.

For example, a priestess from the Temple of Isis glides among the crowd and announces the death of Pharaoh Thutmose III. As she describes which objects and elements played a role in the funeral rites, she explains the long journey that the late pharaoh would take in his search for eternal life. If the death of a pharaoh leaves you cold, you can also experience Cleopatra's last moments with her beloved Mark Antony, or try to understand the motives that led Ramses II to dominate a great swathe of the Middle East in the 13th century BC. The museum also offers a beginners' course on ancient Egyptian culinary treats. The evening ends on the museum terrace, with a banquet of delicacies similar to those that would have been enjoyed by the pharaohs.

The museum has its own study programme leading to a diploma or a Master's degree in Egyptology, as well as educational courses for children and students who are simply interested in the Egyptian world, giving them access replicas of archæological material. Some lectures are carried out in the archæological campus, 20 km from Barcelona in the municipality of Palau-solità i Plegamans. This area has three replicas of ancient Egyptian archæological sites, so students can try their hand at a dig.

Those who prefer to visit the museum in the daytime will find a collection of over 1,000 items divided into five themes: characteristics and functions of the pharaoh, public appointments and private individuals, everyday life, funerary practices, and the world of religion.

MUSEU DEL PERFUM

Passeig de Gràcia, 39

Metro: Passeig de Gràcia
• Tel: 93 216 0121
• Open Monday to Friday, 10:30–14.00 and
  16.30–20.00 and Saturday, 11.00–14.00
• www.museudelperfum.com

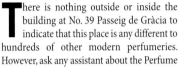

A museum in the back shop

There is nothing outside or inside the building at No. 39 Passeig de Gràcia to indicate that this place is any different to hundreds of other modern perfumeries. However, ask any assistant about the Perfume Museum and they will point out a door at the rear of the shop.

The moment the assistant turns on the lights, there is usually a gasp of admiration upon seeing the display cabinets which some 5,000 perfume bottles, all arranged in chronological order, beginning with censers, perfume burners, and flasks from the ancient civilizations of Egypt, Etruria, Rome and Greece. These relics are the first stop on a comprehensive tour of the history of perfumes, which also includes miniatures, catalogues, and past advertisements and perfume labels.

The museum, open since 1961, holds an extraordinary collection of perfume containers, notable both for their originality and their origins, such as the bottle that once belonged to the French queen, Marie-Antoinette.

The story behind some of the perfumes is also revealed, such as "4711," one of the oldest brands, whose name derives from when Napoleon ordered his troops to number every house in Cologne (Germany), and 4711 Glockengasse was the house of a perfume-maker…

There are collectors' items such as the bottle Christian Dior had made in 1947 for the anniversary of Miss Dior. A limited edition of one hundred bottles was made in Baccarat crystal. There is also a bottle designed by Salvador Dalí for Le Roy Soleil perfume.

SIGHTS NEARBY

GARDEN OF PALAU ROBERT

Passeig de Gràcia, 107
• Metro: Diagonal • Tel: 93 238 4010

At the junction of the busy Diagonal and Passeig de Gràcia is Palau Robert, a centre providing tourists with all kinds of information on Spain. Few know that this late 19th-century mansion has a wonderful garden where you can rest, read, or simply just enjoy the agreeable surroundings. The palace was the private home of the aristocrat Robert i Suris, who commissioned French architect Henry Grandpierre to build him a neoclassical residence.

BARCELONA SEMINARY'S MUSEUM OF GEOLOGY

⑩

Diputació, 231
- Metro: Universitat
- Tel: 93 454 1600
- Open Monday to Thursday, 17.00–19.00
- Admission free

More than just a pile of stones

Located within the Barcelona Seminary, the Geological Museum is an astonishing place where all the guides, directors, and researchers are are Catholic priests.

Despite its tricky access through a maze of corridors and staircases, you should eventually find the museum entrance.

Founded in 1874, the museum specializes in palaeontology, with particular emphasis on invertebrate fossils.

It belongs to the Church of Barcelona and contains over 60,000 items dating from all geological eras.

All of the fossils are of great interest, and a guide who is both a priest and a scientist will explain how and why they preserve the remains of a prehistoric monster found in Sabadell, or why a jaw belonging to a hominid from the Miocene epoch is so valuable.

There is also a library with over 13,000 specialized volumes, and a laboratory for analysing and classifying fossils. Each year the museum publishes its own magazine, Batallería, where activities and new findings are described.

Most visitors are palæontology students and specialists. The priests complain that not many children visit the centre, probably because fossils do not have any gadgets or buttons to play with. In any case, it is advisable to ring before you would like to visit.

If you do get lost on the way to the museum, don't worry, you can always relax on the building's magnificent patios and balconies.

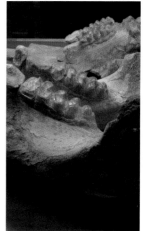

SCHOOL OF SAN MIGUEL DEL SAGRADO CORAZÓN

Carrer de Rosselló, 175
Metro: Hospital Clínic
• Tel: 93 410 4005
• The cloister, in the schoolyard, is closed to the public, so visits should be arranged in advance (or ask the doorkeeper politely and he may let you in)

Stone by stone ...

Saint Michael of the Sacred Heart school is the unexpected home of a three-wing cloister (in the original plan there were four, but one was never built), which was transferred stone by stone from the Raval neighbourhood.

The cloister dates from the 15th century and not only has it suffered dismantling but also a fire during Barcelona's "Tragic Week" (Setmana Tràgica) of church burnings in 1909.

Now its gargoyles are at rest in far more peaceful surroundings, watching benevolently over the basketball games of the schoolchildren.

The reason for the move was the redevelopment of Barcelona's historic city centre two decades ago, in which some buildings and monuments were replaced by public spaces.

The convent of Santa María de Jerusalem, in Plaça de la Gardunya, was one of the victims of this renovation. Its original site is now the car park of the Boqueria market, and what remained of the cloister was moved to the school.

PULLING DOWN AND MOVING OUT ...

Other convents and religious buildings suffered a similar fate. In the 19th century, another great wave of reform within the city's old quarters affected many ecclesiastical properties. At the time, the Church owned close to 20% of the urban area including cemeteries, schools, churches and convents. What was not destroyed in the burning of convents that took place in 1835 and again during the "Tragic Week" of 1909 was expropriated by the city authorities through aggressive legal action. The transfer of the cloister of San Miguel del Sagrado Corazón is only one example of the metamorphosis that Barcelona has undergone in the past two centuries.

The most regrettable loss was the church and convent of Carme, sacrificed in order to widen Carrer dels Angels and give access to Notariat and Doctor Dou streets. The Liceu opera house was built on the former site of the convent of la Mare de Déu de la Bona Nova, while the Orient hotel in the Ramblas is located on land that once belonged to the Franciscan college of Sant Bonaventura. The hotel has integrated part of the cloister into its dining area, where some blind arches can still be seen. The kitchen garden of the convent of San Agustí Vell has been turned into a square, and its library became part of the former Odeon theatre.

THE COMTE D'URGELL TRAFFIC LIGHTS

Carrer del Comte d'Urgell
One at the junction with Carrer de Buenos Aires and another at the junction
with Carrer de Londres

Designer traffic lights

These silver-painted traffic lights on Carrer del Comte d'Urgell have become a symbol of bygone Barcelona. They are the oldest in town, and although nobody is quite sure of the exact date, it is believed they have been set up here since the late 1940s or early 1950s.

The lights are anchored in a block of stone and, to add to their charm, are crowned by a streetlight.

Barcelona's first traffic lights date from the Universal Exposition of 1929, and stood at the junction of Carrer de Provença and Carrer de Balmes. These early examples had to be lit manually by traffic wardens. In later models the light would change when the passage of vehicles activated a rubber device.

During the Civil War, traffic lights were placed at Gran Via, Plaça de Catalunya, Portal de l'Àngel, Passeig de Gràcia, Rambla de Catalunya, and Avinguda Diagonal.

SIGHTS NEARBY

EDITORIAL SOPENA
• Carrer de Provença, 93 • Metro: Hospital Clínic

On the grounds where Ramón Sopena's publishing house used to stand in 1894, there is now a hidden garden. It is one of the few green spaces that has survived the city's urban reforms and was set up as a tribute to the publisher. Artist Jordi Gispert created a curious mosaic using ceramic tiles, sculptures, and other elements he rescued from the building's original façade.

A SODA SIPHON CLOCK
Avigunda de Roma, 105

The concrete siphon at Avigunda de Roma is two or three times larger than life. It contains a clock and hangs outside a vehicle repair shop. The location used to be a factory producing soda siphons (Sifones A. Puértolas), and the present owner decided to keep the siphon clock as a souvenir.

Soda water was a popular drink during the first half of the 20th century. It was often mixed with wine, and was thought to be an aid to digestion. Over the years, the availability of other fizzy drinks, together with the fact that soda siphons were impractical and slightly risky to transport, meant that they disappeared from the market.

AGRUPACIÓ ASTRONÒMICA DE BARCELONA (ASTER)

Carrer d'Aragó, 141–143, 2–E
Metro: Urgell
• Tel: 93 451 4488
• Open Tuesday and Thursday, 18.30–21.00
• www.aster.org

For stargazers

Set up in 1948, Barcelona's Astronomical Association (ASTER) is a select club for those devoted to stars, black holes, comets, and anything else relating to astronomy.

During the 1960s, ASTER members were the first Europeans to tune into the signal emitted by Sputnik 1, employing fairly basic techniques. Since then, the association has acquired an extensive educational role.

One of their most popular activities is the beginners' course in astronomy, open to the public, which explains such things as how to use a telescope and orientation by the stars.

The course includes fieldwork visits to the Tibidabo hillside where you can locate and name the brightest stars.

Venus, Mars, and Jupiter can be seen, and on a clear night 3,000 of the billions of stars in our galaxy can be observed. These night-time excursions last from four to five hours.

There are also daytime excursions to observe the Sun (always carried out with eye-protection equipment).

Students also learn about astrophotography, and will get the chance to take home a magnificent photograph of the moon or a starry sky.

The course costs €110, and places are limited. (The price includes a guided visit to Barcelona's Maritime Museum.)

ASTER also possesses an extensive library and newspaper archive specializing in astronomy, astrophysics, meteorology, and aeronautics, and it is the ideal place to sell or exchange telescopes, accessories, or any second-hand astronomical material.

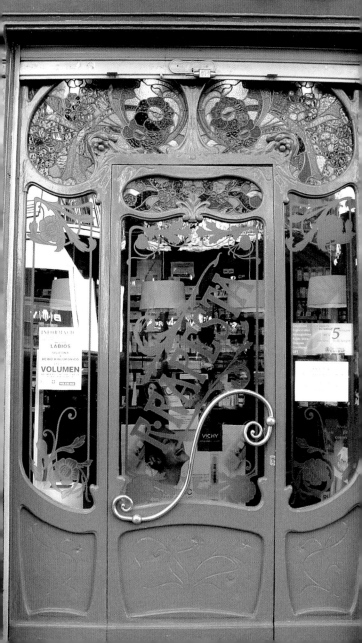

MADROÑAL, FORMERLY FARMÀCIA PRATS ⑯
Carrer del Comte Borrell, 133
Metro: Rocafort y Urgell

Madroñal pharmacy is a masterpiece of Modernist architecture.

The red lantern at the door, which let passers-by know that this place sold medicine, now attracts the attention of children and young people – the shop frontage might have come straight out of *Harry Potter*.

And perhaps this association is not so far-fetched, as the premises were used to brew secret potions based on tinctures obtained from hemlock or gentian, as remedies for apparently incurable diseases.

Although the old flasks now sit among bottles and boxes filled with the latest products of medical science, the pharmacy has lost none of its charm after over a century.

All of its Modernist fittings are original, as are the gas lamps that have been converted to electricity.

The carved ceiling displays the Catalan coat of arms, along with the classic representation of a cup and a serpent; the symbol of pharmacies the world over.

PHARMACIES WITH STYLE

The Madroñal is not the only pharmacy to have preserved its original Modernist decor.

Bolós (formerly Farmàcia Novelles) has also resisted the passage of time. The premises at 77 Rambla de Catalunya, designed by Antoni de Falguera, are in perfect condition.

The same applies to *Farmàcia Mestre* (Villarroel, 53); located in a listed building, it has vivid stained-glass windows and a set of scales from the early 20th century.

Curious visitors will enjoy *Farmàcia Robert* (Roger de Llúria, 74); dating from 1906, it has preserved a device used to sterilize laboratory instruments.

Farmàcia Sánchez (Bruc, 88) keeps a great number of antique flasks and containers, and *Farmàcia Galup* (Pau Claris, 83) has preserved many of its picturesque posters advertising such products as: *"Galup's Cod Liver Oil, the best tonic, better tolerated and the most agreeable to the palate."*

The façade of *Farmàcia Arderiu* (Bailén, 113) has etched decorations and *Farmàcia Enrich* (Muntaner, 83) also has an unusual frontage, its glass and metal door ornamented with the cup and serpent symbol. Inside, antique cabinets display a collection of flasks and bottles.

Similarly, *Farmàcia Sanchís* (formerly Tanganelli), at 117 Rambla de Catalunya, also has remarkable flasks.

Finally, all the fittings at *Farmàcia Vilardell* (Gran Vía, 650) are in carved wood and it still has its antique gas lamps.

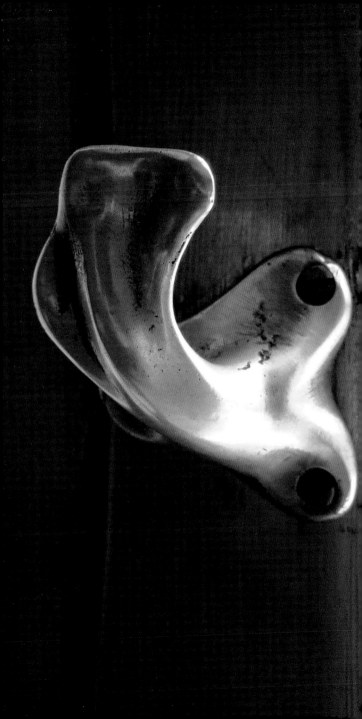

BOX: "MODERNISME" (ART NOUVEAU) IN CATALONIA

The Art Nouveau style began to make its mark in Europe from 1880 onwards and as nationalist sentiment in Catalonia strengthened and drew closer to European rather than Spanish trends, Catalans quite naturally began to adopt "Modernisme", as it was referred to in Barcelona.

In architecture, Gaudí, Puig i Cadafalch, and Doménech i Montaner took the lead in making use of Art Nouveau's æsthetic freedom to create new forms based on nature and revamp traditional techniques.

In painting, the best-known representatives of the movement were Ramón Casas, Santiago Rusiñol, and Isidre Nonell, who habitually met at the Els Quatre Gats café (Carrer de Montsió, 3), which was also frequented by Picasso, whose work of his Blue and Rose periods is considered to belong to this movement.

The name "Art Nouveau" was popularized by Samuel Bing (1838–1905), from Hamburg, who in 1895 opened an art gallery in Paris, called *L'Art Nouveau*, where he exhibited the works of most of the major practitioners of this new art form.

The term *Jugendstil*, used today to describe a particularly geometric tendency, was the original name given to Art Nouveau in Germany and Austria.

A German publisher, George Hirth, launched the satirical review Jugend in Munich in 1896. Its provocative style and original typography were immediately associated with the numerous artistic novelties of the period. Yet other terms were used to evoke Art Nouveau in Europe: *Sezessionstil*, in Austria, designated the Vienna Sezession (separatist) movement launched by Gustav Klimt in 1897. *Stile Liberty* owed its name to Liberty of London, a leading manufacturer of printed textiles, and this word was taken up mainly in Italy and the United Kingdom. Other, less-flattering names, such as *Style Nouille* (noodle style) were used by its detractors.

More than a simple artistic movement, Art Nouveau saw itself as a new mode of thinking, a new way of life, breaking with a model of society that it had rejected. It aspired to emancipate itself from the model of exploitation of working people, the role of the Church and of women, through the discovery of an eroticism and sensuality until then forbidden. Hence the many stylized representations of women's heads on the façades of buildings.

The golden age of Art Nouveau in Barcelona was between 1880 and 1930. In the rest of Europe, it suddenly disappeared after the disruption of the First World War, since it was incapable of producing buildings on a mass scale, yet limited budget. It could not therefore respond to the immense reconstruction needs of the postwar period. In Barcelona, however, the style remained vigorous and there began one of its most fertile periods in artistic terms.

THE SPY SHOP

Carrer d'Aragó, 240
Metro: Passeig de Gràcia
• Open Monday to Friday, 10.00–14.00
  and 17.00–20.30

*Devices
to spy for*

Looking for sunglasses with rear-view mirrors or a device to listen through walls? Perhaps a bug detector or a cigarette pack with a hidden camera?

The Spy Shop, open for almost 20 years now, has every device you could possibly need for spying and avoiding being spied upon.

Some of its star products are a voice demodulator and a telephone the size of a fax machine that can imitate different types of speech: that of an old man, a child, or a woman.

Whether you are interested in joining the paparazzi or simply taking pictures without being noticed, this shop has a full range of options: screwdriver camera, pen camera, cigarette-lighter camera, calculator camera …

SIGHTS NEARBY

CASA DE LA LACTANCIA

Gran Vía de les Corts Catalanes, 475
Metro: Rocafort

Casa Macaya (Macaya house), now an exhibition centre for La Caixa bank, is the work of the great Catalan master of architecture, Josep Puig i Cadafalch (1867–1956).

As a pupil of Lluís Doménech i Montaner, he is considered to be the last representative of "Modernisme" and the first of Novecentismo (a movement seeking to renew standards while reaffirming classical values).

Casa Macaya, built in 1901, offers a superb homage to cycling, the most practical and rapid means of transport at the time. On the capital of one of the columns, Eusebi Arnau sculpted a bicycle. There is a woman astride it, as Arnau wanted to leave evidence of how important cycling had been in giving women freedom of movement and therefore independence.

Although the bicycle is less important today, a network of cycle lanes has been in existence since 1989, starting with a reserved lane on Avinguda Diagonal.

The artist Ramón Casas was himself a great cyclist. Casas and his friend Pere Romeu were the owners of the renowned tavern Els Quatre Gats at 3 Carrer Montsió, where there hangs a reproduction of a famous Casas painting of him and Romeu astride a tandem. The original painting is in Barcelona's Museum of Modern Art.

THE CYCLIST OF CASA MACAYA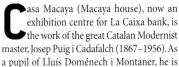

Passeig de Sant Joan, 108
Metro: Verdaguer

*Barcelona
on two wheels*

Casa Macaya (Macaya house), now an exhibition centre for La Caixa bank, is the work of the great Catalan Modernist master, Josep Puig i Cadafalch (1867–1956). As a pupil of Lluís Doménech i Montaner, he is considered to be the last representative of Modernism and the first of Novecentismo (a movement seeking to renew standards while reaffirming classical values).

Casa Macaya, built in 1901, offers a superb homage to the bicycle, the most practical and rapid means of transport at the time.

On the capital of one of the columns, Eusebi Arnau sculpted a bicycle. There is a woman astride it, as Arnau wanted to leave evidence of how important cycling had been in giving women freedom of movement and therefore independence.

Although the bicycle is less important today, a network of cycle lanes has been in existence since 1989, the first of which was in Avigunda Diagonal.

The artist Ramón Casas was himself a great cyclist. Casas and his friend Pere Romeu were the owners of the renowned tavern Els Quatre Gats at 3 Carrer Montsió, where there hangs a reproduction of a famous Casas painting of him and Romeu astride a tandem. The original painting is in Barcelona's Museum of Modern Art.

SIGHTS NEARBY

SPECIAL FAÇADES

Just a few streets from Casa Macaya, at 122 Carrer de Girona, Jeroni F. Granell i Manresa constructed an extraordinary house in 1901 that came to be known as the "humble facc of Modernisme:" *Casa Granell* is a modest building, full of colour and creativity, built for the working class.

Casa Sayrach, at 423 Avinguda Diagonal, is a building of eye-catching organic shapes. Manuel Sayrach (1886–1937) was a fine architect, also active in the fields of literature, politics and philosophy. Most of his creations are personal and imaginative reinterpretations of Gaudí's works.

A few metro stops away, at 106 Carrer d'Enric Granados, is the interesting façade of *Casa Frances Cairó*, a good example of architect Doménech Boada's great talent and imagination.

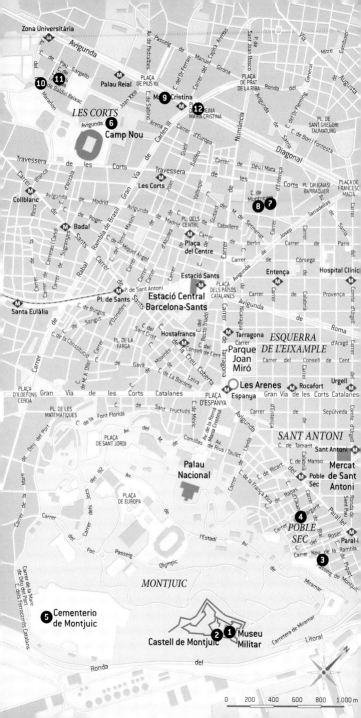

WEST

MUSEU DEL CÒMIC

❶

Castell de Montjuic
Bus 50, 55
- Tel: 658 921 383
- Open Tuesday to Saturday, 11.00–14.00
  and 15.00–18.00; Sunday mornings only
- Admission: €3

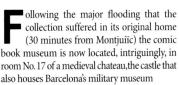

> *Comic book collection in a military museum*

Following the major flooding that the collection suffered in its original home (30 minutes from Montjuïc) the comic book museum is now located, intriguingly, in room No. 17 of a medieval chateau,the castle that also houses Barcelona's military museum

Having made your way through an exhibition space filled with cannons, uniforms, and bayonets, it is quite a surprise to discover a room given over to the life and works of Capitaine Courage or Natacha hôtesse de l'air.

The museum offers a vast collection retracing the history of comic books in Spain, ranging from the first official magazine (Domingín) and the comic strips of the Franco era (Azucena, Florita and Mary Noticias) to the fanzines that managed to avoid the censor on several occasions during the military dictatorship.

At the time ofThroughout the period of the two world wars and the Spanish Civil War the combative theme dominated.

The most popular series was Episodios de Guerra y Hazañas Bélicas ("War Stories of War and Warlike DeedsFeats of Battle"), which included a section encapsulating the general feeling: Semillas de odio ("Seeds of hatred").

Unfortunately the bulk of the archives are still in storage, waiting for a new permanent home.

However, José María Delhom, curator and comic enthusiast, is nearly always available to swap anecdotes about Spanish comics.

If he is not in the military museum, ask for him at the ticket booth.

THE NAME MONTJUÏC ...

... comes from the time when the town was known as *Barcino*, in 15 BC. The hill was known as *Mons Iovis*, which evolved into the Catalan form *Montjuïc*.

In Latin, *Iovis* means "jovial", but the word is also associated with Jupiter – the Roman *dies Iovis* was the day dedicated to the Jupiter cult.

ADVENTURES OF THE METRIC SYSTEMTHE METRIC EPIC

Not many Barcelona residents appreciate to what extent their city was involved in the development of the metre. Nor do many suspect that avenues such as Meridiana and Paral-lel pay tribute to this unit of length, and indirectly to the 18th-century geographers, scientists, topographers, and explorers who carried out the extremely complex observations and calculations required to define it over a period of six years. The task of making the measurements fell to two French topographers: Pierre-François Méchain and Jean-Baptiste Delambre. Delambre was responsible for the northern part of the meridian arc, between Dunkirk and Rodez (France), while Méchain measured the section from Rodez to Barcelona.

Their "geodesic triangulation" technique consisted of tracing a line of triangles whose apexes corresponded to the mountain peaks along the meridian. Méchain worked in close collaboration with two mathematicians appointed by the Spanish king,: José Chaix and Juan de Peñalver. For six years, Méchain and his team travelled with their extremely fragile or extremely heavy measuring instruments, erecting what came to be known as "signal towers,", often in severe weather. They were accused of spying and were almost caught up in a war.

In 1798, Méchain and Delambre met at Carcassonne before returning to Paris with their results, which although, even though they were approved, did not completelyfailed to fully satisfy the Académie Française. So Méchain went back to Spainjourneyed southwards again in 1802, to extending the calculationsmeasurements as far as Ibiza in order to achieve greater accuracy in the definition of the metre. He died from malaria in 1804 and is buried at Castellón. Researchers carried on trying to perfect the unit of length until 1983 (see p. 199).

Pierre François MÉCHAIN

Jean-Baptiste DELAMBRE

SIGHTS NEARBY

MONUMENT TO THE METRE, CHÂTEAU DE AT MONTJUÏC CASTLE

- Bus 50, 55
- Open Tuesday to Saturday, 11.00–14.00 and 15.00–18.00,
  and Sunday mornings. Closed Monday.

In the ditchdry moat to the left of Château de around Montjuïc castle stands a sculpture honouring the metre. *La talla métrica de la natura* ("The metric measure of nature"), by Valérie Berjeron, is a concrete column 9 metres high, set between three trees with different rates of growth: oak, apricot and white poplar. It was sited here because the chateau tower served as a reference point for the measurements carried out by Pierre-François Méchain in the 18th century.

The monument does not get many visitors – few stop to reflect on its beauty andor the achievement that it commemorates.

REFUGE 307

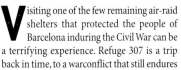

Juntion of Carrer Nou de la Rambla and Passeig de Montjuïc

Metro: Paral-lel

- Open Monday to Friday, 10.00–13.30, by previous arrangement
- Tel: 93 256 2122
- Admission: €8

A historic
air-raid shelter

Visiting one of the few remaining air-raid shelters that protected the people of Barcelona induring the Civil War can be a terrifying experience. Refuge 307 is a trip back in time, to a warconflict that still endures in living memory. The residents of the Poble Sec residentsneighbourhood took refuge there from the relentless aerial bombingardment campaign waged by Mussolini's air forces.

The site was discoveredcame to light by chance during Holy Week 1995, during the demolition of a glassworks that revealed one of the three entrances to the shelter.

Built in 1937, it was one of the best-equipped ofat the time, with electricity provided by a portable generator, an infirmary, sanitary facilities, and water fountains fed by the Montjuïc springs. In theory it could protect 2,000 people from the bombsing, but as construction was never finished the actual number is not known.

Over a period of two years, 1,400 shelters were built in Barcelona, 288 of which were in what is now the Sants-Montjuïc district.

Today, little remains but a few scattered ruins. The renovation of the sewer system and the construction of underground car parks saw the end of most of these shelters. Refuge 307 is one of the rare examples to have survived urban development.

It was also the only shelter not to be closed down by Franco's troops. After the war it was used for growing mushrooms, as storage space for a glassworks, and as a shelter for the homeless. It was closed from the 1960s until its rediscovery in 1995.

Today you can visit the shelter accompanied by a guide who explains the main events of the Civil War and the efforts theby citizens made to create placeshavens where they would be safe from the terror of the bombs.

SIGHTS NEARBY

A STRANGE FAÇADE

Carrer de Margarit, 30

A stroll through Poble Sec can bringoffers some rewarding surprises, such as the allegory of the industrial world on the façade of No. 30 Carrer de Margarit. It consists of a medallion depicting a woman leaning on a cog wheel.

OTHER AIR-RAID SHELTERS

Of the 1,400 air-raid shelters known to have existed during the Civil War, only a few have survived. Most were buried and rediscovered during development work or the extension of the metro.

One of these shelters, at Plaça del Diamant, is a network of tunnels with a sickbay and sanitary facilities. Discovered in 1992 during the renewal of an electricity plant, it is one of eighty-eight88 shelters in the Gràcia neighbourhood.

Work on a new car park at Plaça de la Revolución brought to light another air-raid shelter. It proved impossible to save it intact and only the sickbay and part of the corridor could be recovered. The narrow entrance is by a door within the car park.

In the Caollserola foothills, a millionaire businessman had built a residence named Palau de les Heures. The house stood empty after he died in 1898 until the Generalitat (the autonomous government of Catalonia under the Spanish Republic) took it over during the Civil War. Its shelter is perfectly preserved.

The bunker of the former Soviet consulate, in Carrer del Tibidabo, 17–19, is also completeintact. Inside its concrete walls are several offices, a kitchen, and sleeping quarters, all protected by two armoured doors that can be opened and closed only from withinthe inside. Another private shelter was built in Gaudí's famous Casa Milá. Members of the Unified Socialist Party of Catalonia (PSUC, Partit Socialista Unificat de Catalunya) took refuge there. It was demolished in renovation work in 2000.

A manhole cover in Plaça de Tetuán serves as the entrance to another shelter that remains quite intactin an excellent state of conservation. Also worth a look is No. 6 Carrer de la Fusina, where the sturdy building, now a bar, was an attractive neighbourhood shelter.

Other shelters: can be found at Can Peguera, at Carrer de Sardenya near the Sagrada Família, and the one at Avingunda de Pedralbes, attributed to the formerthe latter used by the President of the Spanish Republic, Juan Negrín, when he resided in Barcelona.

Although these shelters are in excellent condition, they are not all of them are open to visitors, especially without good reasonunless they have special permission.

Many of them are quite hazardous, and can only be entered with ropes and potholing equipment.

To visit the Plaça del Diamant shelter:
Ajuntamentyuntamiento de Gràcia: 93 211 4973

To visit the Palau de les Heures shelter:
Fundación Bosch i Gimpera: 93 403 9100

THE SYMBOLISM

⑤

OF THE TREES IN MONTJUIC CEMETERY

Montjuic Cemetery
Carrer de la Mare de Déu del Port, 56–58
Bus 13, 125
• Tel: 93 484 1999
• Open daily, 8.00–18.00

Funerary botany

Montjuic cemetery was opened in 1883, as theat of Poble Nou cemetery had become too small for the needs of Barcelona residents. The cemetery's 56 hectares of burial grounds here contain 150,000 tombs, some of which are certainly of certain architectural and sculptural interest. At the construction stageIn planning the site, architect Leandro Albareda envisaged an open space with no defined boundaries, in the English style, bathed in light and colour.

Since its conception the cemetery has aspired to aeæsthetic excellence: many of the tombs face the sea and the planting arrangementsations follow the principles of life and death, according to Celestino Barallat, specialist in necrology and author of the unique gardening tome Principios de botánica funeraria ("Principles of funerary botany").

Barallat held that certain plants are appropriate for a cemetery and others leadare conducive to eternal rest. Thorny plants, for example, are banned, with the exception of the white hawthorn, thea symbol of hope, and the wild rose. Nor are cacti acceptable, even though they are sometimes used as a metaphor of fortitude in suffering. On the other hand, you will find plenty of cypress, the magical tree of the Celts and icon of the woods; lawns with few flowers, as intypical of imagery of paradise; swathes of ivy, thewith its yellow everlastingperennial flowers that in Christian iconography herald the revelation of eternal glory; and finally the willow, thea symbol of sadness.

Some of the tombs are magnificent in themselves, especially on the San Olegario, Santa Eulalia, San José and San Francisco paths, where the greatest numbers of works of art to the square metre areare concentrated. There are vaults in marble, bronze, and wrought iron, all sumptuous, as the bourgeoisie spared no expense when interring one of their own. The lavish mausoleums honour some of Barcelona's most illustrious families. and splendid marble figures also honour some great lives. Among the best known are the angels by the sculptor Arnau. There is the spectacular neo-Gothic vault of the Bastinos family, and that of the Urrutia family, neoclassical in white stone. The most well-known or eccentric sculptures include the angels by the sculptor Arnau, another sad angel with his sword and shield on the Serra-Tries family vault, the dreaming angel guarding the Alomar-Estrany family, the lion on the tomb of Alfons Albéniz, and the desperate woman of the Brutau family. The vault belong to the Pomes Casas family even has a carpet.

FC BARCELONA TRAINING GROUND ⓺

Avigunda Joan XXIII, 2–14
Metro: Zona Universitaria
• Tel: 93 496 3606
• Booking required

Watch the next Messi in training ...

One of the rare farmsteads that once lay scattered over Les Corts to have survived the passage of time is the home of the youth team of Barcelona Football Club. The former farmhouse, built in 1702, is located to the east of Camp Nou. Here the football prodigies live, train, study, and count the days before they embark on their professional careers.

Most of them are adolescent boys who have left home and family to dedicate themselves to sport. Their training completely immerses them in the game. Many different nationalities are represented, as well as some boys whose families live in regions far from Barcelona.

Out of this melting pot have emerged players like Guardiola, Xavi, Puyol, Gabri, the Argentine Messi, and many other stars.

The centre displays souvenirs of all the players who have stayed there and who now inspire the next generation of footballers.

The 610 m2 building, surrounded by sculpture gardens, is equipped with kitchen, dining room, living space, library, offices, bedrooms and changing rooms. Of the sixty young players selected by Barça, twelve live here and the rest sleep in rooms at the stadium.

Although you can watch the players training, visits to the centre can only be arranged on request.

Most existing Catalan farms date back to the Middle Ages but they often occupied the sites of fortified farmhouses built by Roman colonists. They usually have massive outer walls and separate wings for keeping animals, but there is no single style and each developed over the years to suit the needs of the occupants. The oldest example is the Masía Torre Rodona, built in 1610 (Carrer de Pío XII, 4).

BARÇA'S COLOURS

Blue and garnet-red have been the colours of FC Barcelona since the club was set up in 1899. These were the colours chosen by the founder, the Swiss sportsman Hans Gamper (who later Catalanized his name to Joan Gamper). His choice was inspired by the football team of Basel, the town for which he had played before coming to Barcelona. Another version of the story claims that he adopted the colours of the Swiss canton Tessin, where his sister lived.

COLONÍA CASTELLS

Passeigs Transversal, Barnola, Piera, Castells and Carrer de Castells
Metro: Sants

*A village
in the city*

Colonía Castells is named after a varnish manufacturing business in Travessera de les Corts. A rural community within the city, its single-storey houses, gardens and terraces are modest but roomy, and above all, very striking.

These houses were built in the late 19th century for the workers who flocked to Barcelona from southern Spain at a time of rampant industrial development.

The varnish factory belonged to Manuel Castells i Carles (1843–1904), who named a passageway after his son, Manuel Castells i Juncosa. He similarly honoured his daughter-in-law, María Dolores Barnola i Grau, naming another alley after her.

The Castells street and passageway, Transversal passageway, Barnola and Piera passageways all preserve the orevious character of this part of the city, but are condemned to disappear, by development plans for a park surrounded by apartment blocks.

For the time being, before it is turned into a building site, you can stroll around this rather picturesque district over 100 years old, still teeming with souvenirs of a bygone age such as the López button factory in Carrer del Morales.

SIGHTS NEARBY

A SHEEP IN LES CORTS

Carrer de Montnegre, 46

Embedded in the façade of some empty commercial premises is a sheep's head carved in stone, surrounded by a garland of leaves, whuch often causes passers-by to halt in their tracks.

There used to be a butcher's shop here and the carving was no doubt made for the Molins family, known as "tripe-sellers", but who also ran an abattoir.

After the Civil War, they closed the abattoir to concentrate on selling tripe in Santa Caterina market.

The only reminder of that time is this strange sculpture, which has become a landmark for local residents.

JARDÍN JAUME VIÇENS I VIVES

Avigunda Diagonal, 629
Metro: Zona Universitaria

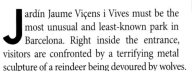

Zoological sculpture garden

Jardín Jaume Viçens i Vives must be the most unusual and least-known park in Barcelona. Right inside the entrance, visitors are confronted by a terrifying metal sculpture of a reindeer being devoured by wolves.

Venturing further into the gardens, other figures of animals emerge, including a family of boars walking in single file, a rather disconcerted-looking deer, and a headless gazelle.

Hardly anyone visits this park to contemplate the beauty of the sculptures, which almost seem to have wandered in by chance. They are made from a variety of materials – marble, plaster, bronze –, without any common style or scale.

Over time, some of the animals have lost various bits and pieces and thus been turned into mutants or hybrids, quite moving to see. This little park hidden in a built-up area is just next to La Caixa savings bank.

SIGHTS NEARBY

HOME WORKSHOPS ON HUMAN EVOLUTION

Hominid Projectes Culturals
Parque Científic Barcelona
Carrer de Adolf Florensa, 8
Metro: Zona Universitària
• Tel: 93 403 4476 / 630 621 930

If you have exhausted all after-dinner topics of conversation, you could always call on the services of Victoria Medina and Silvia Pintado. They organize home workshops on anthropology, archaeology and biology. Their session on human evolution, which lasts an hour, is particularly recommended.

LIFE IN 3D: VIRTUAL REALITY CENTRE

Carrer de Llorens i Artigas, 4-6
Metro: Zona Universitaria
• Tel: 93 401 2591
• Booking required

The virtual reality centre, a joint university and private enterprise project, offers the latest in advanced technology, in particular simulators intended for use by the military (war games) or in medicine (surgical operations). The centre is not normally open to the public, but does receive visits from organizations with specific needs and from keen students.

AN ANALEMMATIC SUNDIAL

Plaça de la Reina María Cristina

Solar time

About 100 metres from the zoological sculpture garden (see p. 139), an unusual type of sundial is set among the paving stones of Plaça de la Reina María Cristina.

This is an analemmatic sundial that works by casting the shadow of a person standing near it.

An analemma is a plot of the position of the sun at a certain time of day at a given place, measured throughout the year. To find the correct time, the sky has to be relatively clear and someone has to stand on the appropriate month.

The person's shadow cast on the dial indicates the hour. This sundial, 10 metres in diameter, was designed in 1997 by Eduard Farré i Olivé and the artistic conception was by Quim Deu. It bears the city coordinates: latitude 41º23'18" north and longitude 2º07'38" east.

The oldest analemmatic sundial still functioning, dating from 1506, is at Bourg-en-Bresse (France).

OTHER SUNDIALS AROUND BARCELONA

There are many other sundials in the city. In Plaça de Lesseps there is a vertical example, carved in stone above the door of Sant Josep's church (known as "Josepts" church). It shows the hours from sunrise to 14.00. Can Tusquets, a farm that serves as a home for abandoned children (Travesera de Dalt, 61), also has a vertical sundial dating from 1793, with Roman figures.

In Plaça du Nord the time is indicated by a rectangular dial 4 metres wide. One of the most original sundials, in Plaça del Sol, is an equatorial dial in bronze set with the signs of the zodiac.

Nearby, at Casa de les Punxes (Diagonal, 418), a ceramic dial attached to the upper part of the façade also serves as a calendar. At Mare de Déu dels Àngels church (Balmes, 78), there is a sundial on each of the four faces of the belltower.

Finally, Bogatell beach by the Olympic Village is equipped with a bifilar sundial in stainless steel and concrete. This type has two threads running parallel to the dial. The intersection of their two shadows gives the solar time.

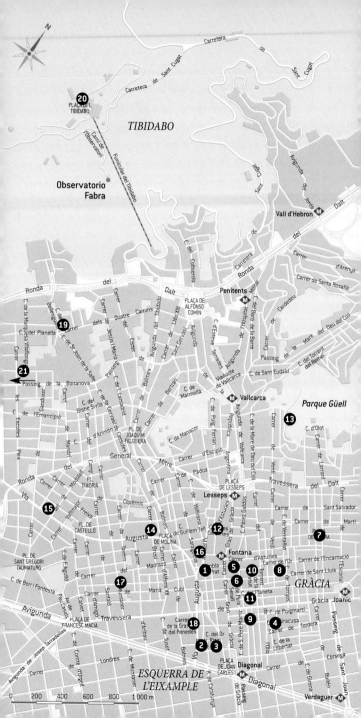

NORTH

THE FOUR FACES OF THE BOSQUE CINEMA ❶

Rambla del Prat, 16
Metro: Fontana

Stony expressions

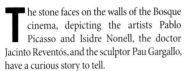

The stone faces on the walls of the Bosque cinema, depicting the artists Pablo Picasso and Isidre Nonell, the doctor Jacinto Reventós, and the sculptor Pau Gargallo, have a curious story to tell.

The site where the cinema now stands used to be part of La Fontana estate, property of Joaquim de Prat i de Roca, which included private woodland.

During the second half of the 19th century a great many theatrical and concert performances were given in this park until finally, in 1905, a theatre was built and named the Gran Teatre del Bosc.

Pau Gargallo was commissioned to carry out the four sculptures that embellish the front of the building. In 1998, after many renovations, it began to be used as a cinema.

The stone faces were also modified but they were retained as part of the conversion.

CHANGING POLITICS: CINC D'OROS

Junction of Passeig de Gràcia and Avinguda Diagonal

The symbolic obelisk at the intersection of two of Barcelona's major thoroughfares has had a very eventful life. Over the course of a century it has been republican, fascist for forty years, and in recent times, monarchist. The obelisk, known as "the pencil" (because of its shape), "the chicken," or "the parrot" (because under Franco it was crowned with the imperial eagle), commissioned from the sculptor Josep Viladomat as a monument to Francisco Pi i Margall, first president of the Spanish Republic of 1873, was erected on 15 September 1915.

On 29 December 1979, the municipality removed the fascist symbols from the monument and placed the royal arms at its foot, in honour of the monarchy. The square, formerly called Cinc d'Oros because it resembled the five coins (*oros*: "golds"), in Spanish playing cards, was renamed Plaça de Joan Carles I in homage to the king.

Passeig de Gràcia, which over the years has become a favourite place to stroll among Barcelona's bourgeoisie, was built in 1821. It was the first attempt to extend the city boundaries and link the Ramblas with the Gràcia district, which was then at some distance from the centre. The route followed a rough track known as *Camino de Jesús* (Jesus' Road). Work was interrupted in 1823 and started again in 1827, to employ men who had lost their jobs during the depression of the 1820s.

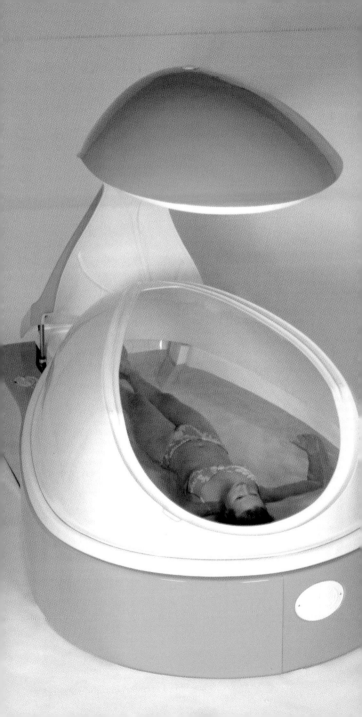

FLOTARIUM

Plaça Narcís Oller, 3
Metro: Diagonal
• Tel: 93 217 3637 • Open daily, 10.00–22.00
• Price: €35 • www.flotarium.com

Like the Dead Sea

As its name indicates, the Flotarium lets you float. The standard session in a container of salt water lasts an hour and takes place in complete darkness. Some say that it reproduces a sensation similar to that of a baby in its mother's womb …

The physical benefits are thought to be many: reduction of muscular tension, improvement in heart and lung function, and strengthening of the immune system. The more sceptical visitor can simply relax and experience a moment of weightlessness in this futuristic capsule.

The Flotarium is an enclosed space of 2.5 by 1.6 metres, containing 600 litres of water and 300 kilos of salts, which gives it a density equivalent to that of the Dead Sea. It is designed to muffle all exterior sounds. You can however leave the door open, with lights and background music on, if you lack the courage for total immersion.

SIGHTS NEARBY

ASSOCIACIÓ BONSAI VILANOVA, TOKONOMA

Carrer del Dr Rizal, 18 • Metro: Diagonal • Tel: 93 415 4040
• Open Tuesday to Friday, 11.00–13.30; Monday, afternoons only

Tokonoma is the only bonsai centre in Barcelona. Exceptionally busy in summertime, when parents often abandon their small charges, it also offers courses on the different styles and methods of caring for these dwarf trees.

PLAQUE OF PLAÇA DEL RASPALL

Carrer de Siracusa, 22 • Metro: Fontana

It is difficult to find the plaque in Plaça del Raspall paying homage to Gato Pérez (Buenos Aires, 1951 – Barcelona, 1990), as it has been fixed to a chimney, of all places.

The square is notable for atmosphere rather than charm. The Gràcia gypsy community often spend time here so you may well come across improvised festivals similar to those once presided over by Gato Pérez, the Argentine creator of Catalan rumba.

Pérez' life was so eclectic that it is no surprise that, among other achievements, he laid the foundations of a musical genre now deeply rooted in the Catalonia. He was butler to an English Member of Parliament, studied physics, wanted to study aerodynamics, drove rally cars, and interested himself in everything, including introducing progressive rock and jazz into the fiercely traditional music of Catalan gypsies.

VITRALLS J. M. BONET

⑤

Carrer d'Asturias, 6
Metro: Fontana
- Open Monday to Saturday, 9.00–14.00
  and 16.00–20.00, or by appointment
- Tel: 93 218 2399
- www.vitrallsbonet.com

Makers of the Sagrada Família stained glass

For almost fifty years, customers have flocked to this studio workshop in the Gràcia district to order stained-glass windows in a variety of shapes and colours. Among the most extraordinary designs that the Bonet family has created since their enterprise was founded in 1923 is the multicoloured glass replica of a dog, commissioned by a Saudi sheikh to decorate his private mosque.

The family has also restored the windows of the cathedrals of Ciudadela of Minorca, Girona, and Seo d'Urgell, as well as the monasteries of Poblet, Santa Creus, and Vallbona de les Monges, while their non-ecclesiastical work includes Gaudí's Casa Batlló. They have also worked with great architects such as Subirachs and Grau Garriga.

Their best-known work, however, is without doubt to be found in the Sagrada Família. Since the 1930s, three generations of the Bonet family have worked on Gaudí's unfinished masterpiece. They made the skylight for the crypt, the windows for part of the Passion façade, and more recently, the transept.

The process of constructing and assembling a stained-glass window is extremely complex. The Bonets first have to import the glass from Germany, Poland, or France.

Then, for the most specialized or valuable designs, they paint them by hand, transfer the design onto a template, and finally cut the glass to shape. The studio specializes in mounting and restoring leaded glass.

The play of light and shadow characteristic of stained glass depends on the thickness of the pieces, in which the Bonets are experts. Part of the charm of this place is that it is one of the rare craft workshops in Barcelona to have survived, along with several others in the Gràcia district.

SIGHTS NEARBY

THE MOSAICS OF LIVIA GARRETA

⑥

Carrer de Pere Serafí, 39 bajo
Metro: Fontana
- Tel: 93 218 3405

The astounding workshop of Livia Garreta is concealed behind a blue door in an orange wall. Inside, yellow, green, blue, red, and violet tones dominate, and the shelves are loaded with the *azulejos* (traditional glazed ceramic tiles) that are Livia's raw materials. From them she creates colourful mosaics in the form of dragons, fish, flowers, or spirals, which are used to decorate paving, friezes, columns, and fountains throughout Barcelona.

SCULPTURE OF ANTONI ROVIRA I TRIAS ❼

Plaça de Rovira
Metro: Joanic

The Eixample that never was

A bronze sculpture in Plaça de Rovira pays tribute to Antoni Rovira i Trias (1816–1889), the architect who in 1859 won the urban design competition for the extension of the city centre.

Rovira was to have been responsible for developing the Eixample. However, a few months after his appointment, the central government in Madrid imposed the plans of d'Ildefons Cerdà by royal decree. Rovira was dropped from the project and had to be content with going down in posterity as the designer of the Corinthian column of Palau Moja, the Gràcia belltower, and San Antonio market.

SIGHTS NEARBY

MOSAICS, CASA RUBINAT ❽

Carrer de l'Or, 44 • Metro: Fontana

Directly opposite Plaça de la Virreina stands the Rubinat house, a building in the Art Nouveau style of the "Modernisme" movement dating from 1909, the work of the prolific architect Francesc Berenguer, designer of other architectural gems in Gràcia, such as the Moral centre in Ros de Olano street or the houses at 61, 77, and 196 Carrer Gran de Gràcia.

The decoration of the façade and the ornamental balconies of the Rubinat house vary in intensity depending on the angle from which they are viewed, the tones changing from red to orange and from orange to yellow, giving the effect of a sunset.

CLIMBING UP THE CLOCK TOWER ❾

Gràcia clock tower • Plaça Rius i Taulet
Metro: Fontana • Tel: 93 291 6615

Not many people know the true history of Gràcia's clock tower and even fewer know that, with a simple phone call and a letter stating your interest, you can climb the steps leading to the belfry and the clock mechanism.

Designed by the architect Rovira i Trias, this 33-metre tower was built to raise the bell so that it could be heard as far away as possible, especially by those churches and parishes that had no bell tower of their own. The bell's peal became notorious in 1870 during a popular uprising against obligatory military service, known as the "Revolta de les Quintes" (revolt against conscription). They also inspired one of the most biting satirical weeklies of the time: *El Campanar de Gràcia*. The clock with four faces that now occupies the tower, so the time can be seen from anywhere in the district, was built by the Swiss craftsman Albert Billeter, who settled in Gràcia and made a reputation for himself with his innovative talent in the art of clockmaking.

FORTE PIANO

Carrer de la Virtut, 13 A
Metro: Fontana
• Tel: 93 237 0787
• Open Monday to Friday, 9.00–14.00 and 15.30–19.00

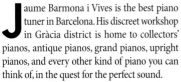

Visit a piano-tuner's workshop

Jaume Barmona i Vives is the best piano tuner in Barcelona. His discreet workshop in Gràcia district is home to collectors' pianos, antique pianos, grand pianos, upright pianos, and every other kind of piano you can think of, in the quest for the perfect sound.

Dismantling a piano and checking each component is like skilled surgery. Most of the time, problems are resolved by changing the filters or adjusting the mechanism.

But considerable finesse is required when a piano is very old and pieces have to be replaced using a type of wood that is no longer readily available.

Forte Piano also offers advice on the styles and makes of piano, and what they are likely to cost. You can call in to ask questions or just to browse around.

SIGHTS NEARBY

A & K ORGUES DE VENT

Carrer del Planeta, 12
• Tel: 93 237 6569

To build an organ, you need to be a carpenter, mathematician, physician, musician, artist, and artisan all rolled into one. In Barcelona, there are only two men who combine all these skills: Antón, who is a native of the Catalan capital, and Klaus, who is German. They are the owners of the only workshop of its kind in the city. They are capable of investing 50,000 hours of work on just one instrument.

The first organ was invented by the engineer Ktesibios of Alexandria in 250 BC. Since then, the technology has considerably evolved, but the time and patience required remain the same. Building an organ to order takes at least a year and costs between 70,000 and 90,000 euros. The main clients are churches, although there are some private customers. Antón and Klaus have recently built an organo di legno (wooden pipe organ). This is a very specialized instrument, made for connoisseurs and costing up to 100,000 euros. They also concentrate on restoring antique instruments. The last time they did this the job turned into a nightmare. The organ, dating from 1791, had to be dismantled in its original setting, transferred to the workshop, reassembled, restored, again dismantled, and finally moved back to be reassembled again in its final resting place.

The workshop is open to visitors, even though Klaus and Antón are not always present on the premises.

CASA VICENCS

Carrer de les Carolines, 22
Metro: Fontana
• This is a private residence, not open to visitors

Gaudí's first work

Casa Vicens was Gaudí's first paid work and first serious project after he qualified as an architect. It is nevertheless often ignored by the thousands of tourists who come to Barcelona to see the great works of the master of Catalan architecture.

The residence was built between 1883 and 1885 following a commission by Manuel Vicens i Montaner. Despite his youth and lack of experience, Gaudí was not in the least intimidated by the responsibility.

He chose to use angles and volumes, in contrast to his future undulating style. Casa Vicens is proof that the master's characteristic style was still developing. In later life Gaudí did in fact affirm that the straight line was man's work and the curve was the work of God.

Casa Vicens is on four levels: a basement, used as cellars; two residential storeys, and the attic for services. One of the characteristics of the building is the colour of the mosaics that decorate most of the façade, giving it a Moorish air. Notable also is the typical wrought-iron gateway in the form of palm leaves.

The building stands next to the convent of the Charity of Saint Vincent de Paul. Gaudí allowed for a large garden area, for which he designed a monumental brick fountain. Unfortunately, this was demolished in 1946 when part of the plot was sold.

The inside of the building, according to those who have visited, is colourfully Baroque.

On the frieze of the gallery, Gaudí had phrases painted that he had written himself, such as *Oh, l'ombra de l'istiu* (Oh, shadow of summer), *Sol, solet* (Sun, little sun), and *De la lla lo foch, visca'l foch de l'amor* (The fire of the house, long live the fire of love).

UNESCO has recently added this example of Gaudí's work to its World Heritage List.

THE CROSSES OF TURÓ DE LAS MENAS

Parque Güell
Carrer d'Olot, 7
Metro: Lesseps
Bus 24 from Plaça Catalunya
• Tel: 93 484 5995
• Open daily, 10.00–19.00

Three mystical crosses

I n Parque Güell, on the hill called "Turó de las Menas", stand three crosses that bear no relation to those of Calvary.

One is in the shape of an arrow pointing both upwards and downwards. The second is oriented north-south, and the third east-west.

Far from being classic Christian symbols, these are tau crosses.

The tau cross was used as a symbol in the megalithic monuments of the Balearic Islands, among other places.

In the shape of the Greek letter *tau*, it consists of an upright stone with a horizontal block on top.

Other similar crosses of architectural importance in Gaudí's work are found in Casa Milá, Batlló, Bellesguard, and at the four corners of Santa Teresa college.

The tau cross is of significance to freemasons, being a sign of recognition in the initiation ceremonies of Masonic masters.

ESOTERIC GAUDÍ

There are many rumours about Antoni Gaudí i Cornet: that he was a member of the Masonic order of the Rose Croix, that he took drugs, that he was a blasphemer, that he was a saint, that he died a virgin, and so on. The theory most often heard and given most credence concerns his links with the world of freemasonry.

According to Ernesto Milá, author of *Guía de la Barcelona Mágica* (Guide to Magic Barcelona), dozens of Masonic symbols can be found in Gaudí's work: the wrought-iron dragon in Parque Güell is made from antimony, the alchemists' metal; the pelican of the Sagrada Família might be there as a tribute to the 18th degree of the Masonic order (final degree of the Rose Croix).

Some quirks of Gaudí's personality did in fact give rise to plenty of gossip. In his early career, he was thought to be arrogant, haughty, and self-opinionated.

As the years went by, however, he became ascetic, very religious (he was a great admirer of Saint Anthony of Egypt, the founder of Christian monasticism), and a follower of the principles of Abbot Kneipp, a German priest, the discoverer of hydrotherapy and a practitioner of what is now referred to as alternative medicine.

Gaudí was very fond of meditating and gave himself up to fasting with such dedication that his usual diet became a few lettuce leaves and endives with olive oil. He gradually detached himself from material things, although the main body of his work was commissioned or sponsored by rich families. He always dressed in an extremely austere fashion.

Gaudí did frequent a number of Masonic circles and his biographers have detected markedly esoteric symbols in his work. For example, the plans of the workers' cooperative at Mataró, for which he drew up plans on a scale of 1:666, recall the number inevitably linked to the Antichrist and the Beast of the Apocalypse. Confronted with these arguments, his defenders have always fallen back on the close relationship he maintained with the Church, denying any links with Masonic lodges.

When Gaudí died it was almost in obscurity: he was run over by a tram at the corner of the Gran Vía and Carrer de Bailén and taken to a public hospital. As he had no means of identification, the medical staff took some time to realize that this gravely injured old man was actually the most famous architect in Barcelona.

GAUDÍ AND PLANT FORMS

Up to thirty varieties of plant are represented in the Sagrada Família. Some, such as the palm tree, have a biblical reference, an allusion to the palms that were laid down before Jesus on Palm Sunday. On the Nativity façade there is a cedar covered in white doves, representing the Tree of Life.

Throughout his life, Gaudí showed a particular interest in cypress trees and took many photographs of them, and they served as inspiration for the Sagrada Família columns.

Mushrooms were also among his favourite forms: there is a small turret in Parque Güell shaped like a mushroom, and in Casa Calvet the balconies are supported by stone mushroom structures. His buildings often reflect the texture and shape of trees, and the way they naturally bend. He liked to analyse the structure of plants, using them not only as decorative elements but also as symbols, and constantly referred to nature in each of his creations.

A MASTERPIECE OF DESIGN

Vía Augusta, 128
Metro: Lesseps

he lobby of 128 Vía Augusta is well worth a visit. This office and residential block, designed by Antoni de Moragas in the 1970s, combines wood, concrete and vividly coloured ceramic tiles. Its extravagant entrance

Barcelona's Clockwork Orange

could well have been the setting for Kubrick's *Clockwork Orange* or one of the retro lounge bars that are currently back in vogue.

Antoni de Moragas (1913–1985), an extremely innovative architect and industrial designer, headed Catalonia's post-war architectural movement and was dean of the Colegio Oficial de Arquitectos de Catalunya y Baleares, the profession's governing body. His work focused on Barcelona's urban development programme and he designed many residential blocks, private homes, and the community centre on Carrer de Gomis. He also supervised the renovation of the Fémina cinema.

SIGHTS NEARBY

VILLA MAYFAIR: A TASTE OF LONDON IN THE HEART OF BARCELONA
Vía Augusta, 240

On one of the city's main thoroughfares, Villa Mayfair is built in the most traditional English style, standing out among other more conventional homes. Its construction fulfilled its English owner's desire to import some of his country's architectural values.

VILLA URANIA: HOUSE OF THE ASTEROIDS
Carrer de Saragossa, 29
Metro: Lesseps

Now a nursery school, 70 years ago Casa de los Asteroides was the home of Barcelona's most distinguished astronomer, Josep Comas y Solá.
A close look reveals an isolated tower in the middle of the garden. This is the observation tower built in the 1920s, allowing the astronomer to study comets, solar eclipses, the planets Jupiter and Saturn, and to discover a total of 11 asteroids (one of which he called Barcelona).
The building, next door to a squat, is simple in construction but very typical of its time, with neoclassical ornamental details.

CLÍNICA BARRAQUER

Carrer de Muntaner, 314
Metro: Muntaner
• Tel: 93 209 5311
• www.co-barraquer.es

For your eyes only

The clinic of Ignacio Barraquer, a renowned ophthalmologist, but also an architect and inventor with a deep passion for design, is unique in the fascinating details it brings out.

Barraquer founded his masterpiece in 1941: an Art Deco building with a metallic structure and rounded forms.

In the foyer, an Egyptian *udjat* (Eye of Horus) protects against the "evil eye" and welcomes patients and visitors, who, if they raise their heads, can check the time from a clock unexpectedly fixed on the ceiling.

The waiting room is round and heavy with symbolism: walls are covered with the signs of the zodiac, Renaissance statues (some of which are decapitated human figures), comfortable leather sofas, custom-made doors and fittings, and mirrors positioned so that their reflections multiply endlessly, creating an optical illusion. (Some of these curious details can be seen on the website.)

Although the Barraquer clinic is visually astounding, paradoxically many of the patients are blind.

It focuses on the investigation, prevention, diagnosis, treatment, and control of all aspects of ocular health.

Although many patients will not be aware of the clinic's visual design details, they cannot fail to enjoy its practicality.

With the comfort of patients in mind, in designing his clinic Doctor Barraquer opted for curved walls, eliminating sharp angles.

He also chose soft lighting, which will not irritate the eyes of patients who have just undergone surgery or recovered their sight for the first time.

SIGHTS NEARBY

A GRENADE IN THE STREET

An iron ball can be spotted on the outside of the wall surrounding No. 12 Carrer de la Granada del Penedès. You may wonder if this sphere, decorated with an iron star on top, is a grenade, a bomb, or simply a metallic ball. Most people believe it to be a grenade dating from the battles between anarchist and utopian socialists in the mid-19th century. This street used to be called just Granada (Grenade) street, but Penedès was added to avoid confusion with another street of the same name in Poble Nou. Fixed to the wall with a metre-long iron structure, the grenade has become a neighbourhood symbol.

TORRE BELLESGUARD

Carrer de Bellesguard, 16–20
Bus 123

Five centuries of inspiration for Gaudí

Built between 1900 and 1905, Bellesguard tower, also known as Casa Figueras, stands in the Collserola foothills on the former site of the castle of Catalonia's last Aragonese king, Martin the Humane. This castle was the king's summer residence in 1410. Five centuries later, it served as inspiration for Gaudí, who insisted on preserving many of the building's original features and its name, Bellesguard (beautiful view).

The brick and stone building, custom-built for María Sagués, widow of Jaume Figueras (hence the name), looks like a fairytale castle.

Viewed from a distance, it could be a scale model or a toy a child has left behind in the garden.

The style is both Gothic and medieval, and unlike most of Gaudí's other works, has no Arab-inspired elements. The defensive tower, crowned with the four-armed cross characteristic of the architect, pays homage to days long gone.

Bellesguard, roofed in green and grey slate, with a great many windows, is divided into basement, lower floor, upper floor, and attic.

The exterior contrasts dramatically with its bright interior, where subtle arcs and soft forms inspired by Art Nouveau are to be found. There is also a 506 m^2 underground water deposit with a storage capacity of 2,000 m^3.

As with the Sagrada Família, Gaudí never completed Bellesguard. Doménech Sugrañes was commissioned to finalize the project, which continued until 1917. Note that visitors are not welcome, as this is a private residence.

MUSEUM OF ANTIQUE AUTOMATS
TIBIDABO AMUSEMENT PARK

Plaça del Tibidabo, 3–4
Bus to Tibidabo departs from Plaça Catalunya
• Tel: 93 211 7942
• Open weekends
• Admission fee: free to €24

*Historic
attractions*

A t the touch of a button, you can activate a miniature ski station, a guitarist, a mandolin-playing clown, or a roller coaster. These are just a few of the most extraordinary devices at Tibidabo's Automat Museum.

They are all collectors' items in perfect condition and date from the late 19th century.

Most of them, such as the tightrope walkers, the guillotine (which demonstrates the precise moment of decapitation), and the mechanics' workshop, are veritable relics of a bygone age.

To visit the museum you need to pay the park's general admission fee, but this is no ordinary amusement park, as most attractions date from the 1970s and have a very different feeling and style to their modern counterparts. Located at the top of Tibidabo mountain, at an altitude of 512 metres (the highest point of the Collserola range), its strange name stems from the Latin tibi dabo ("I will give you"), the words spoken by the Devil in his splendid vanity when he tried to tempt Jesus as they looked down on all the kingdoms of the world. Tibidabo does in fact offer the most spectacular views – particularly on a clear day when the wind has blown away the grey-brown cloud of pollution floating over the city.

When visiting the Tibidabo amusement park, it is also worth checking out the Marionetarium, which gives inventive performances using vintage puppets.

SIGHTS NEARBY

FOSTER'S SCENIC VIEWPOINT

Carretera de Vallvidrera al Tibidabo s/n
• Tel: 93 211 7942
• Guided tours with technical commentary can be booked

Most people will be familiar with Norman Foster's Torre de Collserola, famous from Barcelona's 1992 Olympic Games, but few know that it is possible to gain access to its highest point and enjoy fantastic views of the city, weather permitting. The 288-metre tower is at the top of a natural peak already 445 metres above sea level, which add up to a truly spectacular vantage point. A panoramic elevator travels 135 metres in 2½ minutes to reach the top.

EAST

THE GENERAL'S WATCHTOWER
Junction of Carrer de Crehuet and Carrer de Porto
Metro: Horta

*General
on guard*

(1)

The Horta-Guinardó district of Barcelona is perhaps the least frequented by tourists and the travelling public, yet it has many places associated with interesting anecdotes about the lives of 19th-century locals, such as General Crehuet, an old soldier who lived for many years in a manor house on Carrer de Porto. Within the grounds was a little watchtower fitted with openings through which the general surveyed and guarded the surrounding fields. The tower, at the corner of the narrowest street in Barcelona, is still standing.

A FEW RECORDS
The narrowest street
At the junction of Carrer de Crehuet and Carrer de Porto. The street is 200 metres long, but at its narrowest point, less than 3 metres wide.
The smallest door
No. 10 Carrer del Comerç (La Ribera). Nearby, the rather romantic name of Carrer dels Petons (kisses) originates from the Middle Ages, when condemned men were allowed to say goodbye to their loved ones and receive their final embrace there.
The oldest house
No. 6 Carrer de San Doménech del Call (Barrio Gótico) was first inhabited in the 12th century. The walls have been leaning since the 1428 earthquake.

WHERE DO *ELS QUINZE* COME FROM?
In the Horta neighbourhood many premises, from the poultry merchant to the supermarket, not to mention the lottery booth, are named *Els Quinze* (The Fifteen).
This is also how people refer to part of the Guinardó district, particularly between the junction of Passeig de Maragall and Avinguda de Borbón.
The name refers to the 15 centime fare for the journey between Plaça Urquinaona and Plaça d'Ibiza. In the early 20th century, the tramways had different fares for the various routes. No. 46 cost 15 or 25 centimes, depending on the distance travelled. The conductors rang a bell and announced: *Els quinze*, so warning any passengers who might be tempted to plead ignorance and travel on free to the end of the line.
Tramway No. 46 was inaugurated in 1901 and the route closed on 20 December 1965, at which point a bar owner on Avinguda Mare de Déu de Montserrat named his premises *Els Quinze*.

THE HORTA WASHERWOMEN

Carrer d'Aiguafreda, 10 to 30
Metro: Horta

*Old-style
laundry*

Strolling around Aiguafreda, one of the most typical streets in Horta-Guinardó, it is difficult to imagine that, 100 years ago, the little gardens here formed part of the biggest laundry in Barcelona.

Several metres beneath the streets of Horta-Guinardó, water ran directly from mountain streams. It was so clear and clean that it could be drunk straight from the wells that were part of each Aiguafreda house.

Over three centuries, until the Civil War, the washerwomen did their laundry first with very cold water then with hot water.

The difference in temperature, together with the purity of the water and the women's efficiency, gave the clothes an unequalled freshness and cleanliness when they were sent back to Barcelona.

One of the paradoxes of the city between the 16th and 19th centuries was that the supply of water bore little relation to citizens' needs. Wealthy people often had no water for laundry purposes, nor did they have enough space to lay their washing out to dry.

The water also used to contain a high level of chalk, damaging the smart clothing made by famous designers of the times, much of it imported from Paris.

All this contributed to the development of the Horta laundry service, which employed a great many people.

Every Monday, errand boys were responsible for collecting sacks of washing, piled up at a point between Vía Laeitana and Carrer del Consell de Cent, returning them on Fridays so that the bourgeoisie could dress up in all its finery during the weekend.

SIGHTS NEARBY

BARCELONA'S ONLY PARISH CEMETERY

Carrer de Saldes, 3

The small cemetery beside the church in Carrer de Nazareth is the only one under non-municipal management in Barcelona. With 1,000 plots, it still looks like a village burial ground. The tombs are those of local people, such as Manuel Carrasco y Formiguera, one of the leaders of the Catalan nationalist party, Unió Democràtica de Catalunya, who was shot during the Civil War.

KAGYU SAMYE DZONG

❹

Rambla de la Montana, 97
Metro: Guinardó
- Tel: 93 436 2626
- Open Tuesday, Wednesday and Thursday, 18.30–21.00

The main Buddhist centre in Spain

The main Buddhist centre in Spain was founded in 1977 by his Holiness the 16th Karmapa. It preserves and spreads the teachings of Buddha and is dedicated to the promotion of the physical, mental, and spiritual well-being of its adherents.

The centre belongs to the Tibetan order of Buddhism, Karma Kagyu, and its official name is Karma Lodrö Gyamtso Ling, which means "place of illuminated activity where an ocean of intelligence exists."

The spacious sanctuary has a little shop selling books, incense, figurines, clothes, and various objects associated with meditation and Buddhism.

From time to time, the centre is visited by Tibetan lamas who come to lead seminars on philosophy and Buddhist meditation.

In addition, they offer a variety of courses; for example, on the history of Buddhism in India, or reflections on the seven points of mental stimulation.

Other activities include film shows, yoga classes, courses on different therapies, and the organization of spiritual retreats in the mountains around Barcelona.

In farms far from the city, various types of retreats take place, intended for beginners as well as long-term practitioners. Those aspiring to become lamas undertake retreats lasting at least three years.

There are also weekend retreats, such as that at Ñung-Ne, which develop compassion, one of the five elements by which pupils learn to recognize the play of energy in body and mind; or the meditational retreat, Shiné, which cultivates internal calm.

KARMA KAGYU

The Kagyu lineage is one of the four principal schools of Tibetan Buddhism, the three others being Nyingma, Sakya, and Gelug. The origins of the Kagyu school go back to the teachings of the Indian mystics Tilopa and Naropa, introduced to Tibet by the translator Marpa. Other grand masters of meditation such as Milarepa, Gampopa, and Rechungpa are also associated with this lineage. The Kagyu method is based on the doctrine of Mahamudra (Great Seal) and on meditation. Currently the school has hundreds of centres around the world.

TURÓ DE LA ROVIRA

5

Parc dels Tres Turons
Bus 24, 28, 86, 119

*Remains
of the Horta anti-
aircraft battery*

Offering a superb 360° panorama, Horta's anti-aircraft battery is the best viewpoint in Barcelona. Paradoxically, it was in this marvellous setting that one of the worst episodes of the Civil War took place, the Republican troops having fought to the death here against their Nationalist foes. Their heroic resistance was even cited as an example by Winston Churchill in 1940, just before the Blitz: "I do not at all underrate the severity of the ordeal which lies before us; but I believe our countrymen will show themselves capable of standing up to it, like the brave men of Barcelona."

The air raids by Italian and German forces, supporting Franco's army by systematically bombing the civilian population, destroyed the city. In all, there were 385 raids that dropped 1,500 tons of bombs, resulting in 1,903 conflagrations that killed over 2,700 people.

In addition to Turó de la Rovira, the town has defences against air raids at Turó del Carmel, Sant Pere Mártir, Tibidabo, Montjuïc, Barceloneta, and Poble Nou.

The weaponry consisted of a few anti-aircraft guns and a small fleet of planes, not enough to halt the great offensive. The guns used were mostly of English origin, Vickers 105s built in 1923.

The two types of fighter plane that were most successful in discouraging enemy attacks were the Polikarpov I-15 (nicknamed "the seagull") and I-16 ("the fly"). Both of these Soviet aircraft were acrobatic and versatile, but their guns were not very powerful.

Today, the vestiges of the anti-aircraft battery at Turó de la Rovira and the air-raid shelter have deteriorated because of lack of maintenance and the fact that, until the early 21st century, the surrounding neighbourhood was a shanty town. The authorities have however launched a project to safeguard this site of great historical interest.

ANARCHIST TAXI

- Tel: 620 20 91 20
- Not available on Fridays

The taxi that picks up nudists

An extraordinary taxi service, unique to Barcelona, which accepts stark naked passengers!

The driver, Mariano, naturally enough, applies his libertarian ideas to his service, which he calls the "anarchist taxi." He tries to promote "fraternity, solidarity, self-sufficiency, and direct action, as well as mutual support and fellow feeling."

Frankly, those who would venture into a taxi in the nude are relatively rare, despite the interesting sensation of freedom and independence that the experience no doubt offers…

Once they are inside, the passengers, dressed or otherwise, can choose from the many magazines or comic books on supply. They can also request their preferred type of music.

Mariano likes heavy metal but does not force it on people. He has some pop, salsa, flamenco, and rock CDs available.

To optimize the exceptional service he provides, Mariano also has a selection of toys to keep children amused on the journey, and is willing to transport domestic pets…

If time allows, he can act as a tour guide: he knows the city like the back of his hand and is an expert on the subject of Gaudí's works.

Another of his services is called "Top Blanket." He keeps several blankets in the boot and often asks passengers if they have any to spare. In winter he distributes them to the homeless …

The fare is unbeatable, too. Mariano charges no pick-up fee: his philosophy forbids him from running the meter until a passenger is comfortably installed in his 2001 Mercedes.

Finally, and perfectly logically, Mariano does not always charge for the journey, especially when the clients are non-governmental organizations or involved in projects to combat social exclusion of the poor or other marginal groups.

CAN MASDEU

Camino Sant Llazer s/n Sierra de Collserola
- To book a tour: visitescmd@moviments.net
- www.canmasdeu.net

Community life

This former leper colony in the Barcelona suburbs was abandoned for fifty years until it was squatted in 2001 by a group of young people wanting to experiment with communal living.

Since then, a group of some twenty-five campaigners have been organizing protest actions against war, GM foods, stock market speculation, and the hegemony of the G8, while supporting other squats, and above all, defending nature and community life.

The dynamic is very democratic in that each resident fulfils a specific role or carries out a specific task, always respecting the others' opinions.

They have organized a number of agricultural projects, including an exercise in self-sufficiency that brings together over 100 people to cultivate a plot of land. The aim is to weave community links and produce healthy food by traditional and ecological methods.

The commune also offers courses, debates, workshops, meetings, and the sale of its produce, as well as guided tours.

Although the house is open to the public every day, most activities take place on Sundays. One of the most heavily subscribed courses is agro-ecological education, aimed at children and young people interested in interaction with the cycles of matter, energy, and water.

The spirit of Can Masdeu tends to makes you believe that another world is possible. The group members pollute as little as they can, eat what they grow, travel by cycling, use solar energy and spring water, and recycle their waste into eight different categories.

These people have succeeded in living in harmony with their environment and have even found the time to invent devices such as a washing machine driven by pedal power. They demonstrate their projects to the public with the aim of sharing their way of life, passing on their knowledge, and encouraging imitation. Unfortunately, as with most romantic ideas, Can Masdeu is fighting to survive and the group faces the threat of eviction.

THE SUBMARINES OF BARCELONA

Narcís Monturiol (1819–1885), an inventor of submarines who had little success during his lifetime, has gone down in posterity thanks to his tenacity and vision. Noting the problems faced by coral divers, Monturiol decided to design an underwater vessel. The two-crew prototype, baptized Ictíneu I (from the Greek words for "fish" and "boat"), could not raise enough power to cope with the ocean currents. But the invention worked all the same and Narcís Monturiol was lauded as a Catalan hero.

Next came *Ictíneu II*, much bigger and capable of submersion to a depth of up to 30 metres.

This second attempt was a failure, however, as Monturiol had fitted a steam boiler that heated the cabin to the point of asphyxiating the crew... After many setbacks, *Ictíneu II* was written off and sold. Monturiol, a socialist and supporter of the revolutionary cause, was increasingly misunderstood and lost all hope of attracting funds for new submarine projects. He subsequently devoted himself to developing a machine for rolling cigars as well as building field artillery, but nothing could match his initial enthusiasm. He died without recognition, unaware that Jules Verne had read all his reports before writing *Twenty Thousand Leagues under the Sea* ...

Did Monturiol's work inspire Jules Verne to create the character of Captain Nemo? At first sight, it seems not, as Nemo was rich and Monturiol poor, but closer comparison of their personalities reveals certain common traits.

Barcelona has not wanted to forget the inventor of the submarine and various memorials have been placed at strategic points around the city.

The first is a life-size replica of the Ictíneu, to be found on the Moll d'Espanya in the old port, which was built for the making a film, *Monturiol, el senyor del mar* (Monturiol, Lord of the Sea).

A smaller model, which also appeared in the film, stands in front of the Maritime Museum (Museu Marítim Drassanes, Avinguda de les Drassanes, s/n). At the junction of Carrer de Provença and Avinguda Diagonal is a monument erected in 1963 by Josep María Subirachs, consisting of yet another version of the Ictíneu and honouring the memory of Narcís Monturiol.

DALÍ AND MONTURIOL

Dalí, who like Monturiol came from Figuères, was commissioned to create the Carrer de Provença sculpture. But his demands were excessive: his expenses were too high and he wanted the submarine to arrive by helicopter. So it was finally Josep María Subirachs who designed the monument, although Dalí helped bring the stone from a quarry at Cap Creus on the Costa Brava.

OTHER SUBMARINES ...

On the Bac de Roda jetty by the Mar Bella beach, there stands a restaurant in the shape of a submersible. And the hulk of a real submarine is to be found on the neighbouring Bogatell beach in Poble Nou.

The Hiroshima Peace Memorial Park also features a sculpture in the form of a submarine.

THE CARRER DE SÒCRATES BOMB ⑧

Metro: Sant Andreu

Souvenir of a bombardment

I n the picturesque Sant Andreu neighbourhood, which until less than 100 years ago was a separate village from the city proper, a bomb is embedded in the upper part of a wall. It dates from 22 September 1842, when General Prim took up arms to demand a more liberal government and protest against military conscription.

The Carrer de Sòcrates bomb was one of many that rained down on Barcelona that day.

A bombardment was ordered by Colonel Joaquín Baldomero Fernández-Espartero, was launched from the hills of Montjuïc, but it seems highly unlikely that a missile originating from there could have hit Sant Andreu. Whatever its origin, it weakened the foundations of the building, which was completely rebuilt a few years later in a style reminiscent of Art Nouveau.

During the renovation work, the masons recovered the bomb and attached it to the corner of the new house.

SIGHTS NEARBY

GARDENS IN CARRER DE GRAU ⑨

Between Carrer d'Agustí i Milá and Carrer Gran de Sant Andreu is a street that harks back to an earlier age with its low houses and gardens. At No. 41 you can see a curious collection of multicoloured ceramics, representing some of the sites in the neighbourhood and around Barcelona in a naive style.

LA PRIMITIVA,
BAR & ORNITHOLOGICAL SOCIETY

10

Meridiana, 157

Metro: Clot

• Tel: 93 347 5520

• Open Tuesday to Sunday, 9.30–23.30

"

Beer among the birds

La Primitiva bar and ornithological society opened its doors over 100 years ago and little has changed since. You only have to glance at the shabby walls, the calendars several decades out of date, and the rickety furniture to appreciate the dilapidated state of the place.

Don Antonio, a canary and finch enthusiast, decided to found an ornithological society that welcomed both birds and their owners to either chat or sing.

Over the years, La Primitiva has become a meeting place for the members of this exclusive club of bird fanciers, who come to the bar for an aperitif, a coffee, or a beer, and to play dominos or cards.

Their average age is 60, but this does not detract from the lively atmosphere that promises an original way of passing time.

Every Saturday, birdsong contests are organized on the patio behind the premises. To take part, you only need to pay €12 a year and to keep a canary.

One of the great benefits of belonging to the society is that members' birds can sleep in the bar, so the little creatures are less lonely and will learn to sing along with their friends …

Even though the bar may seem to be exclusively for men, it is open to everyone.

UNIÓN DE CANARICULTORES DE BARCELONA 🕚

Avigunda Meridiana, 91
Metro: Clot
• Tel: 93 232 4204
• Open Monday, Wednesday, Friday and Saturday, 18.00–21.00

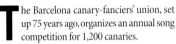

*Karaoke
for canaries*

The Barcelona canary-fanciers' union, set up 75 years ago, organizes an annual song competition for 1,200 canaries. On the day of the contest, as the birds are more at ease singing in the dark, they are separated and their cages covered with a black cloth.

This club of canary fanciers is also the ideal place to find advice on how to improve their song.

A canary imitates other sounds, so if it hears a CD playing first-class songs, its own performance will probably improve.

Similarly, if a poor performer is placed next to a good one, the learner will soon make progress.

The annual competition has three classes: song, colour, and carriage. There are three different styles of birdsong to be judged: *timbrado espagnol*, *roller*, and *malinois*.

As for the colour and carriage contests, the most impressive thing about the show is that you can see for yourself the endless genetic variations between birds.

Some canaries have extravagant feathering and crests, while those entered in the colour class flaunt all the colours of the rainbow.

MONUMENT TO THE METRE

Meridian Arc
Plaça de les Glòries Catalanes
Metro: Glòries or Monumental

Plaça de les Glòries Catalanes was chosen as the site of a monument commemorating the 200th anniversary of the measurement of the terrestrial meridian, which was used to determine the length of the metre. The inauguration ceremony took place before work on the surrounding site was completed, because time was running out for the launch of the 1992 Olympic Games in Barcelona.

The 40-metre steel monument, the work of François Scali and Alain Domingo known as the Meridian Arc, represents the orographic profile (i.e. showing the terrain's relief), to scale, of the distance between Dunkirk and Barcelona.

There is a reason for the length of 40 metres: under the new system, the Earth's total circumference as measured along the terrestrial meridians (or lines of longitude) running from North Pole to South Pole was defined as 40 million metres (or 40,000 kilometres).

Beyond being a tribute to the metre as a system of measurement, the arc is dedicated to all the scientists involved in the definition of the metre using primitive instruments, in particular Jean-Baptiste Delambre and Pierre-François Méchain. On one side of the monument is an inscription describing their work (further details, p. 126).

THE DEFINITION OF THE METRE SINCE 1791

Surprisingly enough, the word "metre" has only been in existence for a little over two centuries.

Before it came into being, there was no standard measurement for calculating distances: hands, feet, or other local units were used.

In 1790, the French National Assembly proposed a universal measurement standard, based on natural phenomena and therefore acceptable to all nations. The chosen measurement was 1/10,000,000 of the quadrant of the Earth's circumference (from the North Pole through Paris to the Equator), to be known as the metre (from the Greek word metron, meaning "measure").

Because it was impossible to measure the entire quarter of the meridian, the solution adopted was to measure part of it and calculate the total. The meridian arc chosen was that between Dunkirk and Barcelona.

After several years of work, a platinum bar was made in 1799. This standard metre, today symbolic (although no longer accurate), is preserved at the Bureau International des Poids et Mesures (International Bureau of Weights and Measures) in Sèvres (France).

In 1875, seventeen countries signed the Metre Convention. In 1889, the Conférence Générale des Poids et Mesures sanctioned a platinum/iridium alloy prototype of the metre that would not be subject to any variations in length. Later, with the advent of laser technology, the same body defined the metre as equal to 1,650,763.73 wavelengths of the orange-red line of the krypton 86 radiation in vacuum. In 1983, a more precise scientific definition was drawn up: the metre is now defined as the distance travelled by light in vacuum in 1/299,792,458 of a second.

MUSEU DE CORROSSES FÚNEBRES

Carrer de Sancho de Ávila, 2
Metro: Marina
• Tel: 93 484 1710
• Open Monday to Friday, 10.00–13.00 and
  16.00–18.00, Saturday 10.00–13.00

*Transport
to the afterlife*

The Hearse Museum is not recommended for sensitive souls. Located in the basement of a branch of the municipal funerary services, it has a collection of various types of carriage and funeral cars from the 19th and 20th centuries.

This is a strange, damp, and rather improbable place. It displays all kinds of conveyances for the deceased, from those decked out in white for children and adolescents to Gothic carriages in the so-called "French" style. Most come complete with mannequins elegantly dressed for the occasion, some in white and others in black. The same applies to the horses, featuring an array of funerary ornaments typical of their day.

Although the set pieces are very well done, it is a pity that the space is so restricted. Nevertheless, there are about twenty vehicles, some drawn by model horses, and showcases displaying the outfits of employees and horses in funerary procession.

This lugubrious, even melodramatic, atmosphere is heightened by the presence of an immense carriage entirely lined in black cloth. This was intended for widows who could afford to pay for lavish funerals, which were mainly reserved for officials or wealthy people, the rare exceptions being burials during Holy Week or at Christmas.

Other striking vehicles include a Studebaker and a 1976 Buick, both of which suggest a less formal style of funeral.

A close look at the exhibits also reveals many symbols linked to death, both in the hearses and on the employees' uniforms. For example, the Greek letters alpha and omega, which symbolize the beginning and the end. Also note the figure of an owl, a symbol of solitude, silence, and death, or that of Athena, the Greek goddess of wisdom, whom we are supposed to meet in the next world. If you want to know more about the death industry, Barcelona's funerary services also run a coffin factory, which you can visit by special arrangement, although it is not normally open to the public.

DIPÒSIT DE LES AIGÜES ⑭

University of Pompeu Fabra
Carrer de Ramón Trías Fargas, 39
Metro: Ciutadella Villa Olímpica
• Tel: 93 542 1709
• Open Monday to Friday, 8.00–13.00; Saturday 8.00–14.00

> *One of the best-kept architectural secrets in Barcelona*

The Dipòsit de les Aigües (Water Deposit) is one of the best-kept architectural secrets of the city. The building, inspired by the Mirabilis Roman baths, was constructed in 1880 by the architect Josep Fontserè.

It was designed as a reservoir for water, hence the vaulted ceilings and brick walls resting on forty-eight pillars.

But over the years it has been used as a retirement home, a fire service warehouse, a film studio, an improvised hospital during the war, and finally, a university library.

In the 1970s, Pompeu Fabra University bought the building, thinking that it was an ideal opportunity to expand its facilities. Architects Lluís Clotet and Ignacio Paricio were commissioned to transform the space and adapt it to the needs of a library.

Apart from the effect of the million books stored here and the powerful architecture, the library has another distinctive feature. Silence is of course the norm, but if you listen carefully, the roaring of lions and tigers can be heard through the huge windows. This is no illusion, the library is next door to the Barcelona zoo.

SIGHTS NEARBY

TÀPIES' CONTEMPLATION ROOM ⑮

In Pompeu Fabra University, a few metres from the library, is a very strange "contemplation room." In this lay chapel, there are no saints or gods to be worshipped, but simply two canvases: *Díptic de la campana* and *Serp i plat*, both works by Antoni Tàpies.

This room, designed by the Catalan sculptor and painter, contains some twenty chairs fixed to the wall.

The original idea was to create a space where visitors could come to terms with themselves, call upon a personal deity, or just admire two brilliant works by Tàpies in absolute silence. If you would like to visit this meditative space, just ask permission at the reception.

POBLE NOU CEMETERY

Carrer de Carmen Amaya s/n
Metro: Poble Nou
- Tel: 93 484 1780
- Open Monday to Sunday, 9.00–18.00
- *Le Baiser de la Mort*: division 3
- *El Santet*: division 1, inner plot 4

Kiss of death

The *Kiss of Death* is one of the strangest tombs in the Poble Nou cemetery. In this masterpiece by J. Barba, a winged death's head is simply kissing the forehead of the deceased. The marble sculpture is a tribute to a dead son. In 1991, it was one of the works most commented on in a Berlin exhibition on the theme of eroticism (!).

El Santet is another strange tomb, with an improvised altar carrying the most surrealist offerings to be seen in the cemetery, such as coffee caramels, cigarettes, and throat pastilles.

Francesc Canals Ambrós (Barcelona, 1879–899), known as "El Santet," was killed in an accident just before his twentieth birthday. Shortly afterwards, the rumour arose that El Santet granted people's prayers. From then on, the number of believers grew and grew, and his tomb is now always covered in flowers and other offerings.

Behind the walls of the Poble Nou cemetery, over 5 metres high, lies a good part of the history of 19th-century Barcelona. The "old cemetery," as the locals call it, is embedded in a traditional neighbourhood that is beginning to give way to modern buildings. It lies almost opposite one of the beaches most popular with young people, Mar Bella.

The cemetery was opened in 1775 in an attempt to solve public sanitation problems. Although now within the urban area, it was originally some distance from the city, outside the walls.

The old cemetery brings together various architectural and aesthetic styles arranged in almost chronological order, and provides a wonderful opportunity to gain some understanding of the personalities and events of another age.

SIGHTS NEARBY

"LITTLE FRANCE"

This small and friendly neighbourhood, home to the Palo Alto Foundation, is known as Little France (*França Xica*), because over 150 years ago, a large number of French employees of a major steelworks settled here. Many of the buildings from that time, however, have been pulled down for housing development projects, although a few streets of rather dilapidated charm remain, such as Carrers de Pellaires and de Ferrers.

THE WATER TOWER SUICIDE

Plaça de Ramón Calsina
Metro: Selva de Mar

Not fit for use ...

Designed in 1882 by the architect Pere Falqués, this historic monument has a macabre story associated with it. One detail was overlooked in the construction of the tower, intended to supply drinking water – the proximity of the sea allowed salt water to infiltrate…

The project was a failure and the devastated investor who had backed it threw himself from the top of the tower.

The system never worked properly and so has remained a monument to human error, inspiring the artists Josep María Subirachs and Ramón Calsina, after whom the square is named.

This tower is important, however, as a tribute to the industrialization of Catalonia and the efforts expended by the workers of the time.

It also forms part of a project to recover the symbols of industrialization.

Over the years, it has become a landmark for the local residents, a playground for the children, and a silent witness to the urban transformation that has taken place, with ever more new buildings under construction.

OTHER RESERVOIRS THAT HAVE SURVIVED THE RAVAGES OF TIME ...

Water towers are used to store water from underground springs or brought in by pipes.

Their height facilitates distribution of the water, sometimes using a pump and sometimes by force of gravity alone. A great many of these towers, most of which date from the early 20th century, have been preserved as monuments to Barcelona's industrial heritage rather than serving their original function.

One of the most remarkable, and the highest (53 m), of these towers is at Tibidabo.

At No. 98 Passeig de Fabra i Puig stands a water tower built in 1910, the property of the Canyelles water company. Nearby, in the Rambla de Sant Andreu, is one of the oldest towers (1853).

Carrer de Peris i Mancheta is home to a water tower built by Josep Oriol (see p. 95), which supplied a journalists' cooperative on Carrer de Roger de Llúria.

FONDATION PALO ALTO

Carrer dels Pellaires, 30
Metro: Selva de Mar

This unusual space, an industrial complex dating from 1875, was renovated in 1987 by Pierre Roca and now houses a foundation dedicated to creative design. The original aim was to avoid destroying the former factories and convert them into spacious, well-lit studios where various artists could work. One of the tenants is the designer Javier Mariscal, whose drawings have appeared on the cover of magazines such as the *New Yorker* and *EPS*. The Mariscal studio employs a team of over forty designers. Palo Alto Fondation has also served as the setting for the film *El Embrujo de Shanghai (The Shanghai Spell)*, directed by Fernando Trueba and starring Ariadna Gil.

THE STONE THAT MARKS AN ANCIENT BOUNDARY

Parque Carlos I

A symbolic stone in the Carlos I park, between Carrer de Marina and Carrer del Doctor Trueta, is in fact one of the boundary stones that used to mark the limits of the municipalities of Sant Martí and Barcelona. The inscription "B i SM" engraved on the stone recalls its original function.
The former village of Sant Martí de Provençals was annexed by Barcelona in 1897.
Vast factories installed themselves in the district, earning it the nickname "Catalonian Manchester."

ALTERNATIVE CONTEMPORARY ART

Hangar
Passatge del Marqués de Santa Isabel, 40
Metro: Poble Nou
• Tel: 93 308 4041
• Open Monday to Friday, 9.00–14.00

The Hangar design centre is located at Can Ricart, an industrial site conceived in the mid-19th century by the architect Josep Oriol y Bernardet. Of the former factory, only a few abandoned buildings remain. Some 250 metres from the entrance, in one of the vast units scattered throughout this phantom space, Hangar set up shop ten years ago and has already survived a fire and several eviction threats. The centre keeps going thanks to the support of the artists' collective, which hopes by this type of venture to prevent property speculation. In fact, after a long fight to establish its rights, it now enjoys the recognition and support of the local authorities.
A visit to Hangar will let you see the latest trends in Barcelona's arts scene and the works of invited artists from all round the world.

SOCIEDAD COLOMBÓFILA DE BARCELONA ㉒

Passeig del Taulat, 7
Metro: Poble Nou
• Tel: 93 266 0210

Federación Catalana de Colombicultura
Córsega, 681, entresol 3º
Metro: Diagonal
• Tel: 93 436 2203

*The world
of pigeons*

For over eighty years, the Barcelona pigeon-fanciers club and federation have been breeding pigeons. The society, with its homing pigeons, and the federation with its racing birds, are almost exclusively for men. Outdoor activities and meetings are organized that revolve around the world of pigeons.

Racing pigeons are by definition aggressive birds: nervous, resilient, and tireless. They are also courtship experts.

Homing pigeons, on the other hand, have very different traits. They are more docile, friendly, and always return to their lofts.

They also have a more athletic body shape. Their breeding and training is very different from that of racing pigeons as they develop an instinct for orientation rather than speed.

The skills of the two types of bird are tested in spring and summer.

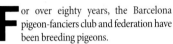

HOMING PIGEONS

Whether released at distances of 500 m or 100 km, and in certain cases, even over 1,000 km, the homing pigeon has the fantastic ability to always find its way back home. Although the reason for this exceptional skill is still unknown, some people attribute the pigeons' gift to the presence of tiny crystals in the brain. This trait was detected a long time ago, notably by Julius Caesar who used homing pigeons in his invasion of Gaul to send messages back to Rome and inform his followers of the campaign's progress.

On the other hand, make no mistake: there is no such thing as the pigeon you sometimes see in films, which is released to take a message somewhere and then returns. The pigeon is only (so to speak) capable of journeying homewards. This is why, in order to send a message to several different places, pigeons raised at each destination have to be taken out. To carry several successive messages to the same place, the requisite number of pigeons would be needed ε There's nothing at all miraculous about this, and moving pigeons from one loft to another will make it difficult to pick up your messages ...

ALPHABETICAL INDEX

ALPHABETICAL INDEX

THEMATIC INDEX

BARS, RESTAURANTS, HOTELS AND SHOPS

CURIOSITIES

GARDENS AND WALKS

MUSEUMS

SCIENCE AND EDUCATION

Acknowledgements
Our thanks to:

María Antón, Alexandra Barba, Josep Baucells, José Bauer, Manuel Bauer, Fiorella Battistini, Elena Bort, Lluís Casamitjana, Melissa Chiarella, Yaki Creiger, Trinidad Delor, Alejandra Devéscovi, Giselle Etcheverry, María Galaxia, Nabila Giha, Nicolás Giha, Camila González, Francesca Goytisolo, Carlos Granés, Fietta Jarque, Helena Liñan, María del Mar López, Eva Morla, José Muñoz Reales, Marianella Muro, Mutualde Conductors, José Pérez Freijo, Silvia Pérez López, Olga Perucho, Iu Pino, Carlos Ramírez, Mali Ramírez, Rufina Redondo, Isabella Reich, Lola Repiso, Natasha Rigas, Craig Sanders, Vicenta Sebastián, Fernando Sierra, Meritxell Tellez, Morgana Vargas Llosa, Juan Miguel Varón, Manuel Vázquez, Manuel Villate.
Hotel Omm, Hotel La Florida.

Photo credits:

All photos by Rocío Sierra Carbonell and Jacques Garance, except:
BARRIO GÓTICO. Santa Agata: Museo Histórico de la Ciudad. Museo Marés: Natasha Rigas. Huellas Prostitutas: Verónica Ramírez. San Cristóbal de Regomir: Mutual de Conductors
EL BORN – BARCELONETA. Celler de Macondo: Alejandra Devéscovi. Escultura Erótica calle Mirallers: María Galaxia. Amigos del Ferrocarril: Juan Miguel Varón. Mano Barceloneta: Juan Miguel Varón
EL RAVAL. Buzón limosnas: Vicenta Sebastián. Cine en casa: Natasha Rigas
EIXAMPLE. Biblioteca Arús: Natasha Rigas. Museo Egipcio: Museo Egipcio. Semáforo Design: Vicenta Sebastián. Aster: José Muñoz Reales. Farmacia modernista: NatashaRigas. Ciclista casa Macaya: Natasha Rigas
NORTH. Cine Bosque: Juan Miguel Varón. Flotarium: Flotarium. Bellesguard: Natasha Rigas
WEST. Refugio 307: Pepe Herrero. Colonia Castells: Natasha Rigas
EAST. Garita del general Crehuet: Natasha Rigas. Turó de la Rovira: Juan Miguel Varón. Los submarinos de Barcelona: Mali Ramírez. Carrer Grau: Natasha Rigas. Unión Canaricultores: Natasha Rigas. Sociedad Colombófila: Natasha Rigas

Cartography: Cyrille Suss
Design: Roland Deloi
Layout: Michel Nicolas
English translation: Caroline Lawrence
Proof-reading: Tomas Clegg
Cover: Romaine Guérin

In accordance with regularly upheld French jurisprudence (Toulouse 14-01-1887), the publisher will not be deemed responsible for any involuntary errors or omissions that may subsist in this guide despite our diligence and verifications by the editorial staff.

Reproduction, even partial, of the contents of this book by means of any media whatsoever is forbidden without prior permission from the publisher

© JONGLEZ 2008

Registration of copyright November 2008 – Edition 01
ISBN: 978-2-9158-0739-4

Printed in France